KNEAD to KNOW

the Real Bread starter

Real Bread Campaign
realbreadcampaign.org

BREAD

Contents

Foreword

Whether you are a professional baker, a home baker who would like to turn a hobby into a career or just someone who loves Real Bread, then this handbook will become an invaluable tool. It contains advice, recipes and insights from some of the most experienced members of our trade: bakers, millers and retailers. We have all learnt our craft through years of experience, through trial and error and occasionally even by making mistakes, dusting off the flour and starting again and now you have the opportunity to learn from all of that massed experience.

For my own part, I believe there is something addictive about flour; that something magical happens when you mix flour with water. With good ingredients, passion and this handbook by your side you can master the dough, learn the language of bread and continue on your journey as a successful Real Bread baker.

Richard Bertinet

Real Bread Campaign ambassador, Richard Bertinet, award-winning author of Dough and Crust, founder of The Bertinet Kitchen & Bakery and BBC Food Champion 2010

Portrait by Jenny Zarins

Introduction

So, you want to be a successful Real Bread baker for your local community. Well, here's a good place to start.

Beyond tips on setting yourself up to produce and market tasty loaves of Real Bread successfully, Knead to Know offers some answers to questions including:

- What are the opportunities to forge and strengthen links with my local community?
- How can I make a healthier loaf?
- In what ways can I reduce the negative environmental impacts of my business?

Who is this for?

As bringing Real Bread back into the hearts of our local communities and food economies is a key concern of the Campaign, we concentrate on small-scale production and newcomers to the exciting world of professional baking. Even if you are up and running already, you will find this guide contains information that should be of use, such as suggestions for marketing your Real Bread, for example.

Will Knead to Know tell me everything I need to know?

This isn't a bread bible, a recipe book, nor does it aim to be a comprehensive manual to starting your own business. Instead, it is a buffet of tasters with pointers to where you can explore and find out more about the topics you find the most appetising.

Importantly, reading is no substitute for rolling up your sleeves and getting stuck into the dough. In Real Bread making, you learn some of the most important lessons with your hands in your own bakehouse. Also extremely useful is spending time alongside an experienced professional, either on a course or better still as an employee or voluntary apprentice at an artisan bakery.

We've enriched Knead to Know with thoughts from people who know how to knead. You can find out who they are in the Roll of Honour section near the back.

If you have advice from your own experiences that you feel would be of use to other people in the growing Real Bread community in Britain, which you would be happy for us to help you share through our website and publications, such as any future editions of Knead to Know, please email realbread@sustainweb.org

BREAD

About Real Bread

The state of bread in Britain

Sadly, long gone are the days when every loaf came fresh from the local bakery or home oven, made with nothing but natural ingredients, time and care. Today, around 80% of bread production is controlled by a small handful of companies, churning out millions of wrapped, sliced, additive-laden, Chorleywood Bread Process loaves each day from remote and highly automated factories.

The Chorleywood Bread Process (CBP) was devised by the British Baking Industries Research Association, based in the Hertfordshire town from which it takes its name. Developed in the aftermath of the Second World War to reduce our reliance on imported grain to produce fluffy loaves, and unleashed in 1961, CBP replaces natural fermentation time with high-speed mixing and higher levels of yeast than traditional recipes to inflate the dough. The mix is laced with a whole range of chemical additives (and increasingly, added enzymes), which perform a variety of functions, including making the dough conform to the stresses of the process; to become stretchy to rise high and quickly and then to tighten up to stay risen; and help the finished loaf to stay softer longer. We will look at the issue of fermentation time in the section below and the matter of additives in the next chapter.

Supermarket in-store bakeries account for a further 15-17% of 'bread' production, but even many of these loaves are baked using similar additives and methods (a process called Activated Dough Development) in out-of-town factories, before being transported around the country to be baked again in stores' 'loaf tanning salons' and then sold as fresh.

The Real Bread Campaign

The Real Bread Campaign is part of Sustain: the alliance for better food and farming. The Campaign's key aims are to encourage people to eat more locally produced Real Bread.

Membership of the Campaign is open to everyone who cares about the state of bread in Britain. Some join as individuals, others on behalf of Real Bread bakeries, independent mills, schools and other community groups.

The Campaign is funded by the Big Lottery Fund's Local Food programme, which supports local food projects in England. The Campaign also receives funding from the Sheepdrove Trust and in the form of subscription fees from Campaign members. We also welcome donations, which can be Gift Aided.

For more information on the Campaign please visit www.realbreadcampaign.org

Campaign members can join The Real Baker-e online forum and anyone can sign up to Breadcrumbs, our monthly e-newsletter. For the latest news and snippets, follow @RealBread on Twitter, or click 'like' at www.facebook.com/realbreadcampaign.

What is Real Bread?

Everyone has their own idea of what Real Bread is, so for the record, the Campaign defines it as made with:

- Flour
- Water
- Yeast (bakers' or naturally occurring)
- Salt

NB - Certain flatbreads don't require yeast and a few types of bread, notably from Tuscany, don't use salt.

Additional ingredients are great as long as they are natural (e.g. seeds, nuts, cheese, herbs, oils, fats and dried fruits) and contain no artificial additives.

Importantly, making Real Bread does not involve the use of dough conditioners, flour 'improvers', processing aids, chemical leavening or any other artificial additives.

As a starting point, this is Real Bread that is accessible to all.

Better bred bread

Beyond our basic definition, we are finding ways of making bread:

- Better for us
- Better for our communities
- Better for the planet

Please read on to find out how.

Longer fermentation

Although not in the Campaign's basic Real Bread criteria, we encourage a longer dough fermentation period. Real Bread is a natural product and just as with fruit or cheese it takes time for it to ripen. There is growing evidence that leaving dough to ferment for longer periods can have a range of benefits to the consumer. Research so far has been limited and we call for much more, but so far studies have reported:

- Improvement of mineral bioavailability, that is to say, changes in mineral compounds which allow the body to make greater use of them.
- Reduction in the gliadin fractions (components of gluten) responsible for triggering gluten intolerance and coeliac disease.
- Reduction of phytate levels – phytic acid reduces the body's ability to absorb certain nutrients from food, such as calcium, magnesium, zinc and iron.
- Reduction of acrylamide in baked bread – a suspected carcinogen, acrylamide occurs in carbohydrate foods cooked at high temperatures i.e. fried, roasted or baked.

It seems that the beneficial effects listed above may be more pronounced in breads produced by longer fermentation in the presence of lactic acid bacteria (LAB), for example in genuine sourdough (see the *Notes on Real Bread recipes and methods*). In addition:

- LAB can lower the glycaemic response to bread, which has positive implications in terms of diabetes and obesity.
- The acids act as a natural preservative, enhancing the keeping quality of the bread.
- The by-products of sourdough fermentation include many compounds that add to the strength and complexity of the flavour of bread.

You can read more on these issues and references to relevant research in the FAQs section of our website.

The importance of time

By Campaign co-founder, Andrew Whitley

Bread making is essentially the transformation of flour and water into a different, more edible, state by the application of various forms of energy over time. This transformation usually involves the biological process of fermentation, whose by-products include the gas that aerates the structure of leavened bread.

Time is an essential component of this process. It allows yeasts (either present in the flour or added) to produce carbon dioxide gas, while, given long enough, naturally-occurring lactic acid bacteria have an effect on the proteins in the dough and contribute to bread flavour, texture, nutritional quality and digestibility.

Bread can be made in a great variety of styles and shapes, but the underlying objective to render flour and water appetising by trapping gas in the structure and then baking a crust around it – is constant. The Real Bread baker's skill lies in working with the natural properties of simple foods (like wheat and rye) and allowing time for natural processes to deliver the best possible results.

By contrast, chemical and enzyme-based dough-modifiers (the likes of 'improvers', emulsifiers and flour treatment agents) replace both the baker's skill and time by manipulating the physical and chemical structure of dough to a uniform specification, without the need for significant fermentation. Such additives are excluded from the Campaign's definition of Real Bread because:

- They are either derived from substances that play no part in healthy human nutrition (i.e. they are not foodstuffs) and/or they are biochemically manipulated for functional effect, with potentially negative effects on human digestion.
- Their use almost always circumvents the process of prolonged fermentation, which is required to deliver the optimum benefits of the bread to those who eat it.

Get Real!

Here are some of the reasons people want locally-baked Real Bread. As you are reading Knead to Know, chances are that you have decided to follow this path already but we include this chapter in case you need a hand in sharing some of the benefits with potential customers.

The desire to enjoy all-natural food

Countless generations eating Real Bread have proven beyond any doubt that it is safe for the vast majority of people. By contrast, artificial additives only undergo a relatively short period of testing before being declared safe - or in the more pragmatic terminology of the US Food and Drink Administration, 'generally recognised as safe' – before being let loose on the market.

What has not been tested in any controlled way is the effect on the human body of long-term consumption of the cocktail of artificial additives we ingest in endless permutations. Sometimes it might feel that we are participants in some sort of mass experiment.

Worryingly, what is declared safe today, might not be considered so tomorrow. History is littered with chemicals used in food production that manufacturers defended, but were then forced to withdraw due to public pressure or a change in law: think of azodicarbonimide, benzoyl peroxide, Agene and chlorine-based bleaching agents for bread flour, all vouchsafed by scientists and the food industry but then dropped (or banned) due to concerns of effects on health ranging variously from impaired endocrine function to neurological disease. The International Agency for Research on Cancer even listed one, potassium bromate, as possibly carcinogenic to humans.

Understanding that consumers can find lists of chemical name or E numbers off-putting, increasingly manufacturers are turning to processing aids. This is a category of substances (usually added enzymes) that can be used in food production, but do not need to be declared on the ingredients list. Suppliers often market these as 'clean label' or 'label friendly'. Read more at www.realbreadcampaign.org.

Better for us

A Real Bread bakery within a local community can offer people some or all of the following benefits:

- Increased access to healthy, all-natural loaves.
- Organic loaves, which may be lower in potentially harmful petrochemical residues.
- Products made with flours of higher nutritional value and levels of dietary fibre than refined roller-milled flour.
- High quality products that elevate eating beyond mere necessity to a pleasurable activity.
- A shorter commute for its staff than to a distant factory, which could have positive psychological effects.
- A job that involves a high level of manual skills, which could be more rewarding than a day monitoring computers and machines.

We didn't expect for people to be quite as excited about the bread as they have been. Sometimes it feels almost like we're providing therapy in a warm paper bag.

Dan McTiernan

Also see the notes in the first chapter (*About Real Bread*) on the possible health and nutritional benefits of longer fermentation.

Better for our communities

Between the 1950s and 2000s the number of small (fewer than eight employees) local craft bakeries plummeted from 18,000 to around 3,500[1]. Not that we deny any industrial baker his or her job but we believe that a local craft bakery is of greater benefit not only to its bakers but also its local community.

These included:

- A higher ratio of employment to product more jobs-per-loaf than a factory.
- An opportunity for social interaction.
- Money spent with local suppliers is more likely to be re-invested locally.[2]
- Helping to support local producers, growers or other smaller or more ethical suppliers by providing an outlet for their goods.

In addition, a bakery may choose to take on volunteers or apprentices, offering them new skills and work experience that could be used in other settings and possibly help them get paid employment.

The network of beneficial relationships we've established between other businesses and within the community has meant that money is not the deciding factor. Good will and the wish to see a real bakery back in the community is a real driving force!

Dan McTiernan

Better for the planet

The following are steps that we encourage all bakeries to consider taking:

- Providing an outlet in the heart of a residential area, making it easier for people to shop by foot or by bike.
- Reducing packaging and choosing reusable (e.g. offering customers a bag for life – bag for loaf?) and/or recycled materials that are also fully biodegradable.
- Using organic ingredients, which have had a lower (or zero) input of petrochemical fertilisers, pesticides, fungicides and herbicides.
- Using flour from local mills, ideally produced from locally-grown grain using truly renewable sources of energy – e.g. wind or water power.
- Working to reduce your energy consumption at all stages of production – the Carbon Trust can help with this.
- Opting for 'greener' sources for as much of your energy as possible, such as wood and biomass from sustainable sources, or better still fully renewable sources – wind, water, solar, hydroelectric etc. Using biodiesel from recycled cooking oil (not from crops that could have been used as food or from land that could have been used for food production or was once rainforest…) to power delivery vehicles.

We take our responsibility to minimise the impact of the business' day-to-day operations on the environment very seriously, as outlined in our environmental policy: thethoughtfulbreadcompany.com/environmental_policy.php We have a commitment to reducing resources, reducing, reusing and recycling wherever we can. When we started, virtually everything was second-hand, from our ovens and mixers, down to bread tins, wall coverings made from old plastic advertising signs and a shed built from wooden palettes in which we kept the recycled cooking oil that powers our delivery van.

Duncan Glendinning

The varieties we grow produce very long stems and are ideal for thatching roofs, and the grain makes great bread, so we hope that this will reduce the amount of straw and grain the country has to import. In the future, we hope to open our own bakery selling the Oxford Loaf. We also hope to encourage more local farmers to grow our crop and more bakers to bake with our flour. We are hoping to run workshops about preserving the biodiversity of our cereal crops, and encourage more local people to become more involved in the growing, harvesting and baking of their daily bread.

Sally Lane

Quality and taste

Quality and taste are both subjective: everyone has a personal set of criteria for each. A Chorleywood 'Bread' Process (CBP) baker would undoubtedly protest that his/her loaves are of the highest quality, whilst a couple of generations with access to little but CBP may well have learned to prefer the taste (or lack of) to the unfamiliar flavour of Real Bread. And it's not just consumers - typically, a British baker will have been taught that uneven-shaped loaves, large, irregular holes and a tangy flavour are all the signs of failure, quite the opposite to many continental counterparts.

In general, our customers were similar to us in that they were persuaded to part with £2 or more for a loaf, not because of some technical reason like the bread's Glycaemic Index or micronutrient bio-availability, but because they were won over by the flavour - once they got used to the different texture (and that they need to chew a bit) they were hooked.

Sue Tennyson

As a Real Bread baker you are well advised to listen to other Real Bread bakers, your customers and your own instinct to help you satisfy yourself that you are baking the tastiest, best quality loaves that you can.

You then need to shout from the rooftops that you are doing so!

Minimising food waste

Obviously, you will take steps to minimise wastage, both in your ordering and production. These include:

- Market research to determine probable demand for different loaves.
- Looking at daily, weekly and seasonal buying patterns, and adjusting output accordingly.
- Ongoing promotion of your business and products to help them sell.

If you do find yourself with leftovers, your options include:

- Can dough offcuts that are too small to be made into loaves be made into rolls to sell or perhaps even pizza bases for staff meals?
- Any flour left on work surfaces, inside proving baskets etc. can be swept up, sieved and kept in a container for dusting.
- Bread left at the end of the day can be recycled as new products. If your bakery includes an eatery, consider adding bread and butter pudding, bruschetta, or maybe panzanella to the menu as daily specials when necessary. Otherwise, try something simple that can be taken away – e.g. dried as real breadcrumbs, fried as croutons, or made up as bread pudding or treacle tart.
- Finding a local project that makes meals for those in need and that will take your leftovers.

Here are some organisations that will collect food waste and use it to feed people most in need of a decent meal. There might be others local to you.

www.fareshare.org.uk
www.foodcycle.org.uk
www.foodchain.org.uk

A trail of breadcrumbs from your kitchen

In this chapter, Paul Merry looks at the journey from amateur to professional baker.

Becoming a busy amateur can be very rewarding and satisfying. It usually involves the physically punishing process of trying to produce many loaves from the inadequate facilities of a domestic kitchen, the most glaring hitch being a too-small oven. Often I have been wide-eyed with admiration listening to one of these amateurs on the cusp of becoming a professional, describing how in preparation for their monthly farmers' market they work in their kitchen for the whole day and night before the market day, perhaps snatching a couple of hours' sleep before loading the back of the car and heading off to claim their pitch.

Taking the step from being an amateur to a professional can be a slow and steady affair, or a big leap. When it is slow and steady it is usually neighbourhood-centred. You start off just baking for a few friends but soon you find yourself providing bread to half your neighbours. Then you get a stall at a local market, your bread is admired and before you know it, you are supplying a village shop or two and your nearby farm shop. If the momentum keeps going, soon you will be challenged to start reducing the hours you do at your normal job.

I baked for myself for many years, then started supplying local markets more or less by accident. Although I don't make big quantities, I'm currently supplying a deli and a café, and looking at upping the oven count from one to three. The large influx of visitors into West Cornwall makes it viable, but I also supply quite a few people in my home village.

Steve Rickaby

To go from amateur to professional takes quite a bit of courage, a fair bit of money and a huge amount of energy! I've been doing this for three years now and only just feel like I know what the customers want and that I'm on the right track.

Being business-minded helps, but we're not and we've managed!! We were lucky in that we bought a shop with a lot of the basic equipment that we would need (including an oven, a mixer, racks and tools) already there and part of the purchase, and that helped enormously. Taking over an existing business can help in other ways, as you already have customers that you just need to convince to stay with you. The first few weeks are manic, and you will make a few mistakes, but if the bread is good enough people will come back.

Feline Charpentier

Homebakeries

The domestic kitchen nightmare can be viewed as a good testing ground. Not only does it test resolve and commitment but more importantly it also shows the need for consistency. I would think the main challenge to the small craftsman is to be consistent. If you have been knocking out large amounts from inadequate facilities and managed some level of consistency, you are half way there. In escalating the business by finding bigger premises and investing in a better oven and some real bakery machinery, you will easily achieve the consistency required of the professional craftsman.

Our personal motivation for making some decent bread came about after a trip to Denmark and the discovery there of the most fantastic looking and tastiest bread we'd ever had! Literally 20 or 30 different types of bread, each with incredible flavours and textures - something for everyone! Truly, having tasted that sort of bread you simply can't go back to the rubbish that's churned out here, so we started making some for ourselves at home and we were off...

Sue Tennyson

Employing a baker

Others go into professional baking by taking the big leap. While tinkering around at home they realise how much they enjoy the baking, and being at a cross roads in their life, or being soundly discontented with their working life (such a person may be a fine example of one going through a 'mid-life crisis'), they take the plunge, romantically opting for being a small scale baker because there is a host of feel-good factors about a small bakery. If they have sufficient wealth to be able to employ a professional baker at the start-up phase, I still say to them that it is wise to learn as much as possible in a short time about fermentation and bread, because they have to be able to judge not only their final products, but also the skill and worth of their baker.

Going it alone

Many will decide to take this giant leap knowing all the way that they have only themselves to rely upon, that the sum total of their limited wealth and finance dictates that they will work alone. Here I urge the baker to attend some courses, and try to pin down a job for a while in a bakery so that the scale and rhythm of a working bakery can be experienced and understood. Often on my own courses I meet such a potential baker and I sometimes have a continuing relationship with them, helping with the start-up phase. However, I always stress the wisdom of getting a job in a bakery for a while.

Becoming a Real Bread baker is a lifestyle, not a career choice.

Aidan Chapman

The right stuff

Whether you are one who has taken the giant leap, or one who has gradually emerged from amateur to professional, there are things in common. It helps to have such a passion about bread making that you are forever chasing after 'the perfect loaf'. If you wish to be a craftsman, working with your hands and minimum machinery, then in order to become excellent at your craft you must have this yearning and aspire to making your best bread day after day, forever chasing after excellence. If, on the other hand, you are driven more by the goal of earning a good living, or building a brand/name that you can franchise, then the passion to chase the elusive perfect loaf is not essential in your make-up. Instead you will have to have the passion to understand and quickly master the nuts and bolts of the business side of high quality and small scale baking.

One thing I must emphasise: opening a bakery is such a commitment. In the process many will find out how difficult it is to make money this way. Baking is anything but glamorous. It nearly killed me! You cannot think by going on a course or reading some books that you are prepared. You will learn in time and get better in time. But be prepared to suffer lots of nights with little or no sleep, a decrease in social life or a lack of money. Is it worth it and would I do it again? Hell yeah!

Troels Bendix

Enthusiasm over skill. You have to be able to get up to bake, then get out there and sell it. Skill you will learn, and have to learn quickly.

Tom Baker

Retail vs. wholesale

During the process of moving from amateur to professional, you may find yourself confronted by a choice between being a retail establishment, or a wholesaler. Retail tends to involve the expense of being on the high street or in a designated shopping centre, with formidable rents and high commercial rates, but does mean that you will be a personality in your own shop, having a relationship with your customers. Wholesale usually involves less expense for premises, often being on an industrial estate or in an out-of-the-way place. While at a glance the set-up and running expense is less, there will be the expense of a delivery van and its driver. Further, when you are working with your hands and aspiring to be a craftsman baker, it really hurts to give away that 20-25% that is the accepted wholesale rate.

Start small

In the early days of being a professional baker, I think it is wise to start small. Give yourself time to get the hang of being a baker who is learning skills. By doing the same tasks every day you will gradually increase your efficiency and pick up speed. When the business is going well enough for you to think the workload has become something of a nightmare, employ another baker, get more help in the busy shop. The same goes for machinery. At the start-up phase when you need to concentrate on becoming a decent baker you should keep machinery to a minimum.

With fewer machines you are going to handle the dough more and intrinsically learn about fermentation and your chosen craft. Later, you can select certain machines that will enhance the output of your already good bread and pastries. For small scale crafters, remember 'alternative technology' is there for you: you can get superb pastry rollers that have a crank handle, not an electric motor, and there are good manual bun presses available that can stamp out 30-odd buns or rolls at a time without the electric rotating head facility. Actually the hand finished buns and rolls will usually be better than the ones from the electric rotary press, which often manages to mangle them to some degree.

My approach is that instead of getting dough hooks and other machinery when the project seems to grow beyond our limits, we need more kneaders - more hands. It seems a shame to give to a machine work that is so satisfying and meaningful and good for body, soul and planet. Lately when my wrists have been a bit sore from over use, I've been getting volunteers from a neighbouring recycling project to come for an hour and knead the dough. In return, later I take some beautiful bread, warm from the oven, to them at their workplace.

Pilar Lopez

Get a life

In the 'lifestyle' area, it is difficult to strike the right balance between night work and day work. If you do not like working at night, staff may help, because you do meet employee bakers who prefer to work at night. Another thing to consider would be to educate your customer base to shop for their fresh bread in the afternoon and evening because your bakery is a morning place not a night place, with most of the goods coming out of the oven during the afternoon. This pattern is easier for wholesalers who are less governed by the tyranny of retail shoppers.

We always knew we didn't want to be night bakers, partly because we had a young child and partly because we didn't want to miss out on sunlight! We currently start at 5am on week days and 4am on Saturday.

Dan McTiernan

I definitely recommend keeping it to one day a week!! During Thursday, I refresh my stored starter from 200g to up to 3kg and then spend from about 10 until 12pm that evening mixing and kneading the sourdoughs, as well as preparing the sponge for the yeasted bread. These are then left to ferment overnight - 7 to10 hours, depending on ambient temperature. At 6am on Friday, I light the wood-fired oven, followed by shaping and proving dough from 7 until 10am. From 10am-1pm I bake the sourdough loaves in the wood oven. I make my rye and yeasted bread during Friday morning and bake using a regular gas oven.

Tom Baker

Market research

Do not be careless or hasty in selecting the location for your new business. As we hear over and over nowadays, location is so important, and getting it wrong could quickly kill your business. A craftsman needs appreciative customers who are prepared to pay more for the hand-crafted product. You will not survive if you are entirely surrounded by typical British shoppers who want all their food at the lowest price possible. If the public passing your door is muttering 'look at those prices, I can get it for half that at the supermarket', then clearly you have set up in the wrong area. There has to be an adequate ratio of 'foodies' in the neighbourhood to ensure success, whether you are retailing or wholesaling.

The Campaign's encouragement away from roller milled white flour is okay, but you also have to judge your market. There's no point in churning out wonderfully ethnic loaves if 80% of your potential customers refuse to eat anything other than white bread. As my personal contribution to the alimentary health of west Cornwall, I have put a lot of work into wholemeal recipes, but it's still a minority taste. The café in my village, for example, won't use wholemeal rolls with their ploughman's lunches because the customers won't eat them.

Steve Rickaby

See the *Marketing* chapter for more on this subject.

Can you grow too quickly? Is there a size limit? When do you say stop?

The answers to all of these depend on your priorities and the reasons that you are baking Real Bread. If you're in it for the money and your definition of success is centred on generating more profit than the year before, then perhaps the answers will be 'no, no and never', respectively.

Alternatively, your key drivers might include philanthropy, a creative urge, or your environmental conscience, and you may decide that a slow and steady growth to a level at which you are breaking even or turning only a small profit is the way forward.

We have a small community of small producers. Quite a few of those small producers are under constant pressure to up their output and supply more. Most, if not all of us, have declined to do so. One reason for this is, of course, time, as for most of us what we do is a part-time activity and subservient to some other occupation. But another key reason, and this is my point here, is the cost of upping output. We have all established methods of working, and in many cases upping output would involve abandoning that way of working in favour of something else, often with substantial capital costs. Or it could mean taking on an assistant, with all the overheads that brings.

Having said that, our marmalade and pesto lady recently bought a big RoboChef machine, and I'm trying to pluck up my courage to buy two more ovens and install them in my conservatory, the only place possible, but I'd rate up-scaling as one of the major challenges for small food producers.

Steve Rickaby

This is really important. Yes you can grow too quickly! Don't do it! Burn out is a real risk. There is such a demand for good bread that if you said 'yes' to everyone you would collapse in a heap within six months. Be honest with yourself about what you need (financially, socially, family-wise....) and don't compromise that. We have had requests to supply food service business that make sandwiches for British Airways and Marks & Spencer, as well as from two supermarket chains, and we could have expanded to be at least ten times bigger than we are currently within the first 18 months of baking. If that's what you want, then great, but that was not our own goal.

We set out to provide Real Bread for our local community and to create at least two livings out of it, but already we have gone beyond that. To date, we have created the equivalent of three full-time jobs, spread between nine people, which makes it sustainable for all of us. There was a point, however, at which Johanna and I were doing nearly everything on our own and this was very tiring and mentally and emotionally draining. Now we have others involved, it is much more rewarding and energising.

We believe in finite growth and are unconcerned that this is swimming against the current capitalist thinking for business. We are happy to have a small thriving bakery that is making enough loaves to make it financially stable without compromising quality of bread and happiness of employees. Beyond that, we are not interested. Any growth for us would then be sideways into other interesting sister projects, such as more education or wheat growing.

We also have a 'kitchen table' rule with business partners and customers, which is to say that we only work with people we would be happy to invite into our home and share food with round our kitchen table. This has stood us in good stead so far!

Dan McTiernan

Cinnamon
Danish
80

Kicking the additive habit

Some thoughts from Paul Merry for bakers looking to make the transition from chemically-enhanced loaves to Real Bread.

You are already in business, and you are attracted to changing to Real Bread, which entails having the courage to introduce a different style of bread to your customers.

Be up front and talk to them, and publicise your change of direction - most shoppers really appreciate being taken into the shop owner's confidence. Consider the kudos in such a move. The customers will appreciate your dedication and sincerity about creating real food. Remember the edict from France that has been broadcast since the advent of industrial post-war food: all you need to make good bread is flour, water, yeast, and salt. Pure simplicity. With your choice of natural stoneground flour it becomes healthy simplicity. Most customers will be grateful to experience this freedom from 'dodgy' chemicals, about which we hear so much nowadays.

As you begin to make bread with less volume and possibly a slightly firmer crumb, extol the virtues of its chemical-free status, its honesty, its value as the staff of life. Make a song and dance about the simplicity of wholesome bread only needing flour water yeast and salt. And also point out that it makes much better toast.

Technically, these are the main things to look out for:

- Expect a loss of volume without the gluten-enhancing additives, and possibly a less glamorous bloom on the loaf. In short, they will look different. Go with it, don't fight it. If you try for big volume you will have over-proved and dry bread. You may have worse to deal with – bread prone to collapsing as it is led to the oven.
- Without added yeast foods (such as sugars or chemicals used in industrial processes) the final proof will be slower, simply requiring patience and adjustment of your schedules. On days when schedules have gone haywire because you are very busy, the final proof will be abnormally long because the bread has been somewhat exhausted by sitting too long in bulk or at intermediate proof.
- There may need to be minor adjustment to life style issues: longer dough time may mean longer hours, a different start time, re-arrangements with key staff. These are all minor problems and certainly worth it for the distinction of elevating your bakery to the ranks of Real Bread.
- Without chemical additives the types of bread that you have always made quickly to suit your schedule may now, as Real Bread, stale slightly quicker. You may then be led to explore other methods of bread making that lead to improved moisture retention – longer fermentation, sponge and dough method, and sourdough (see *Notes on Real Bread recipes and methods*).

All of this is an exciting challenge, and surely stems from your original decision to rise to the primary challenge of changing to Real Bread.

Making the switch Q&A

With answers from Peter Cook.

Will producing Real Bread increase my costs?
Possibly in terms of labour but other costs will be reduced as you won't be using expensive concentrates and bread mixes.

What adjustments do I need to make to production scheduling and will I/my bakers need to work longer hours?
It's a fact that Real Bread takes longer to make. But by learning and experience you can increase the fermentation times to suit your schedule. Someone may have to come to work in the evening to mix overnight doughs, but that can be rotated to suit the bakers.

Can I use my existing flour?
Probably, but the best results will come from working with the best flour you can. Try using a local mill with which you can develop a good relationship.

Do I need new special equipment to make Real Bread?
No, although you may need to think about containers in which to store dough while it is fermenting.

I don't think that my customers will like sourdough, so how can I make Real Bread?
Real Bread is not necessarily sourdough but for any new product, try making small batches at weekends first - that tends to be when customers are looking for something a bit different. When it starts to sell in larger numbers, extend the production into the weekdays.

Will my bread look or taste different?
It should taste a LOT better. Slow fermentation brings with it a whole new level of flavour. Much Real Bread will be baked on the oven floor rather than in tins, so there will be more crust.

Can or should I charge more for these new Real Breads?
You must work out how much they cost to make including labour costs. Then charge what you think your market will stand. People

are prepared to pay more for Real Bread, although how much more will depend on your local trading conditions. You need to get the message across to your customers about how your bread differs from that bought from the supermarket.

What other implications (positive and negative) are there for switching to Real Bread?

By testing the skills of your bakers, you will be giving them a challenge. By meeting that challenge, they will attain greater job satisfaction.

I was the first bakery in my area preaching Real Bread and this has played a significant part in establishing my business within the community. Our customers' expectations of anything we make is that it will be of a high standard because of the dedication we impart in the production of our breads.

Moving away from 'improvers' can be a great way to re-focus your business as there is such a lot to communicate to the customer. Since I started baking Real Bread, I find that a greater number of customers have increased their knowledge of bread and are now asking quite searching questions.

Although supermarkets will win on price, they cannot compete with the quality and range of products a craft baker can offer. Once they see this, understand what we are doing and why, and taste the products, I find more customers are willing to pay extra for Real Bread.

Paul Barker

Who can help me make the transition?

The Real Bread Campaign has enlisted the help of a host of Bakers' Angels, who include some of the country's leading artisan bakers. If you have a question, post it in The Real Baker-e forum, where answers should not only help you, but also other members. You might also find that your flour supplier is happy to provide advice and assistance or works in association with a baker who can help you move to Real Bread.

Ingredients

Flour

As the main ingredient of Real Bread, this is the most important building block of your loaf. In this introductory guide, we will only look at wheat flour, from which the vast majority of bread baked and eaten in the UK is made.

Although the type of flour used is not a criterion in the Campaign's basic definition of Real Bread, we encourage the use of higher extraction (i.e. a greater percentage of the grain ends up in the flour, with true wholemeal flour being 100% extraction) stoneground flours, preferably produced from organic grain that has been grown and milled locally.

Extraction rate

This is the percentage of the de-husked and cleaned wheat berry that makes it into the flour sack. Wholemeal flour should be 100% extraction (though see the note below on stoneground vs. roller milled flour); British-milled white bread flour will be around 72-75% extraction (though it may be lower in traditionally stoneground flour) and brown flour will fall somewhere in between, usually 80-85% extraction. Continental millers use different systems of classification.

This information is rarely shown on bags of flour for domestic use but a miller or professional bakery supplier will be able to tell you what you are getting.

Protein

Britain has a love for high-risen loaves, with small even-sized holes in its crumb. To produce this type of bread, you need to use flour with a relatively high percentage of protein - around 12-14%. The type of protein is also important - such British-style loaves require strong flour with protein that will stretch well without breaking.

The characteristic lower volume and large, uneven holes in continental-style breads are made possible by flours that have lower protein levels and/or weaker types of protein.

For advice on the appropriate flour to use, tell your miller or flour supplier the type of bread you are making.

Organic ingredients

The number and amount of toxic petrochemical herbicides, fungicides, and pesticides used in growing grain in a lower input system of farming (such as organic and biodynamic) will have been lower than in 'conventional' systems. The amount of petrochemical fertilisers will also have been lower. Some organic and biodynamic farmers will have used no artificial substances at all.

This will all have had a lower negative (and in some cases an actual positive) impact on the health of the soil, surrounding water systems, and lead to fewer and lower levels of potentially toxic chemical residues in the food chain.

www.pan-uk.org
www.soilassociation.org

The question of which is 'better' - locally-grown in a 'conventional' system, versus organically grown further afield, is complex and one that the Campaign doesn't attempt to answer.

Stoneground vs. roller milled flour

Modern roller milling is ruthlessly efficient at stripping away the nutrient-rich germ and outer layers of cereal grains, leaving behind a white powder that's not much more than starch and gluten. When adding the separated parts back together to make 'wholemeal' flour, a roller-miller might exclude the nutrient-rich germ.

Instead of removing the outer layers of the grain, stone milling crushes the grain and all parts are mixed in together. Even when sifted to produce a lower extraction (lighter coloured) flour, it will still contain fine particles of the fibrous and most nutritious parts - the germ and bran. There has also been research to suggest that the heat generated by roller milling destroys greater percentages of nutrients in comparison to stoneground flours of equivalent extraction rates.

Amongst the studies that have shown the difference between the nutrient levels in whole grain and roller milled white flour, one from the US Department of Agriculture listed depletions that included 70% of the iron and 93% of the vitamin E[3].

Even though almost all UK milled bread making flour has to be 'fortified' by law (see note below) there is still a whole range of minerals, vitamins (including vitamin E), antioxidants and phytonutrients (phyto = plant) that are not replaced at all during fortification.

Flour additives

The Bread and Flour Regulations 1998 demand that calcium, iron and vitamins B1 and B3 are all added to white and most other UK milled bread making wheat flours, except wholemeal. These do not have to appear on the label. As this fortification is mandatory, our 'no artificial additives' criterion has to have this one exception.

When purchasing flour, always check the ingredients list to make sure that the mill has not added any 'improvers' or other non-mandatory artificial additives. This even applies to organic flours.

A common 'improver' is ascorbic acid, otherwise known as vitamin C. This is harmless (but not nutritionally beneficial in bread – baking renders it inactive) and found naturally in citrus fruits. However, it is not essential and in its highly refined or synthetically produced forms, it is no longer a food ingredient, but an additive not permitted by our criteria.

See the bread labelling page at realbreadcampaign.org.

Local loaves

Is there an independent mill in your area? By using their flour you will forge a personal link in the chain from seed to sandwich, help to support local employment and the local economy, and minimise the energy used in transporting the flour. If it is a traditional wind or water-powered mill, the energy used in milling will be non-polluting and you will be supporting local heritage.

Better still if the grain has been grown as locally as possible, too. In addition to the benefits above, local supplies and stores of grain are much more resilient to interruption by factors such as adverse weather conditions, industrial action and fuel shortages, which have more opportunities to have impact on transport systems in extended chains.

See the marketing chapter for ways in which local provenance can be used as a sales tool.

Using British flours

As Nick Jones points out at the end of this chapter, some flours milled from 100% British grain can be weaker than those produced from imported wheat. If you intend to produce a loaf with a weaker flour, you have two options: finding or developing a recipe that works with its characteristics (perhaps a crumpet, focaccia-style or flat bread) or experiment with mixing it with different ratios of strong flour. If choosing the former, take full advantage of the marketing opportunity this gives you – a loaf that is special or even unique to you.

Leavening

The Real Bread Campaign's definition includes breads leavened with naturally-occurring yeasts (as found in a sourdough starter - NB true sourdough cannot be called yeast free!), fresh bakers' yeast or dried active yeast. Unleavened (e.g. flat) breads also meet our criteria.

If considering using instant (also known as fast acting, easy blend or easy bake) yeast, to keep it real, you will need to read the label and avoid brands containing artificial additives: almost every brand we've found (including some organic lines) contain them.

Chemical leavening

As it avoids the biological process of fermentation, chemical leavening (e.g. as is used in soda bread and scones) falls outside the Campaign's definition of Real Bread - perhaps someone else would like to start the Campaign for Real Soda Bread…

Salt

In bread baking, salt helps to:

- Enhance the product's flavour.
- Strengthen the gluten network.
- Aid the browning process – bread with lower levels of salt may appear paler, whilst high levels may cause a reddish, 'foxy' bloom to the crust.
- Act as a natural preservative, delaying the onset of mould growth.

Due to its anti-microbial properties, salt also has an effect on fermentation. Lower salt levels will allow faster and higher rising than higher salt levels.

You may prefer to use rock or sea salt, but pure table/cooking salt will give you the same results. Always check the label, as many brands contain one or more anti-caking agents – sodium hexacyanoferrate, for example. Such an artificial additive would put your loaves outside the Campaign's definition of Real Bread.

Salt and health

With our 'better for you' hat on, the Campaign supports the use of lower levels of salt than many industrial loaves contain and, indeed, some craft bakery recipes call for. The Food Standards Agency (FSA) website states:

"In the UK we are eating far too much salt, and high salt diets result in high blood pressure, leading to an increased risk of heart disease and stroke. So the Agency is working successfully with industry to reduce the levels of salt in 80 categories of food to help reduce people's daily intake. We have set a voluntary salt reduction target for bread of 1g salt /100g final product by 2012."[4]

For this reason, the Campaign recommends a salt level of no more than 1% of finished product weight.

To help bakers calculate how much salt to use in order to ensure that their finished products contain no more than 1% salt by weight, the FSA has created an online calculator:

www.food.gov.uk/news/newsarchive/2010/jul/bakers

You can read more about the health issues related to salt a the Consensus Action on Salt & Health (CASH) website:

www.actiononsalt.org.uk

Fats and oils

Fats and oils added in appropriate amounts can be used to perform a number of functions in both plain and enriched doughs. These include contributing to the textural/structural characteristics of tenderness (as in the opposite of toughness), moistness, increasing dough extensibility (and so allowing greater volume) and slowing the effects of staling. Fats and oils can also be used to contribute flavour by their own taste, helping us to taste fat-soluble flavour compounds, and by assisting browning.

Palm oil / fat

Generically labelled 'vegetable' oil, fat or shortening may well be partly or all from palm, a relatively cheap source. Critics including Greenpeace have raised concerns around the sourcing of palm oil and fat[5]. The main issue is that they believe that certification systems are either not rigid or policed well enough to be able to guarantee that palm oil has not come from a plantation cultivated on cleared rainforest land. You may prefer to check with the supplier of any 'vegetable' oil or fat to ensure that it doesn't contain any palm at all.

Saturated and trans fats

A diet high in saturated fat and/or trans fats is linked to raised levels of blood cholesterol and an increased risk of coronary heart disease[6]. Saturates are found in high levels in animal fats (e.g. butter and lard) and hydrogenated and partially hydrogenated oils/fats, including some shortening and margarines. Small amounts of trans fats are found in butter, but in higher levels in partially hydrogenated oils/fats.

Reducing or doing without

Andrew Whitley suggests that to achieve maximum loaf volume, you need no more than 5g of fat per 1kg of flour (more for wholemeal), whilst higher hydration of the dough will contribute to tenderness, extensibility and slowing of the effects of staling. As fats and oils are not essential ingredients of Real Bread, unless an intrinsic part of a recipe (e.g. butter in brioche) for the above reasons, you might consider eliminating them from your loaves altogether.

How and why should artisan bakers work more closely with traditional mills?

The Traditional Cornmillers Guild is giving Britain's old windmills and watermills a new lease of life at a time when the sustainable qualities and clean self-renewing power of wind and water are being valued again. Guild Chairman, Nick Jones, reflects on possible new opportunities for Real Bread bakers:

Traditional mills are much more than specialist food producers and an important part of Britain's rural heritage. The majority of the Traditional Cornmillers Guild members are small businesses run by dedicated individuals, families, volunteers, local authorities and charitable trusts. Very often they play an important part in the local community, provide employment, generate sustainable power, preserve old rural crafts and skills, contribute to the tourism economy, and offer an invaluable educational resource including tours, training, and milling, baking and bread-making courses. Many work closely with nearby farmers and use locally grown grain. Most supply a range of flours and cereal products, often milling to individual needs, for example milling wheat, rye, barley, spelt and other specialist flours.

Up until Victorian times, white flour was considerably more expensive and difficult to produce than coarser, browner flours, and was therefore more likely to appear on the tables of the wealthy. The introduction of high speed roller milling powered by steam (and later electricity) combined with the increased availability of strong high protein wheats from warmer, sunnier climates including North America and Australia was good news for British bakers, and for the larger millers. The stronger, whiter flours absorbed more air and water than the softer, heavier homegrown grains, and were less susceptible to the vagaries of British weather. The British public took to the lighter, softer bread although it was often less tasty and, in spite of nutritionists' worries about lack of fibre.

So, why is traditional milling better, and how does it differ from modern milling? The key is in the way the grain is ground. The simple grinding of the whole grain in a single pass through and between two horizontal, round millstones is at the heart of traditional milling. It is designed to produce wholemeal flours with excellent flavour and nutritional value. The bottom stone, called the bedstone, is stationary, and the top stone, the runner, rotates. The grain is fed through a hole in the centre of the runner, the eye. It is ground into flour as it takes a few seconds to move outwards between the two stones. Nothing is taken away in the process – whole grain goes in, and wholegrain flour comes out so the flour retains its integrity.

And that is the point. In its whole state, grain contains a natural balance of starch, protein, vitamins and fibre. In wheat, many oils and essential B and E vitamins are concentrated in the wheat germ, the life force of the grain. The oily, flavoursome and nutritious wheat germ cannot be separated out in stone grinding, so its gets spread throughout the flour, and provides its delicious, characteristic nutty flavour.

In contrast, modern mills are specifically designed to produce white flour. They use a series of high-speed rollers that scrape and remove a layer of the grain, sieve it off, then remove another layer, and so on. A particle of flour can travel over a mile during this process – passing between rollers and sieves. It enables the wheat germ and bran to be removed efficiently and has the capacity to achieve a high level of extraction and to produce a vast amount of flour quickly and with minimum human intervention. The considerable heat generated in the process of roller-milling can affect nutritional quality, and a 2005 French study observed that sieved stoneground organic flour had a significantly higher zinc and magnesium content than an equivalent sample of roller-milled non-organic flour. It is possible to produce roller-milled brown flour by re-integrating and mixing the various sieved components, but it is not the same as stoneground wholemeal.

For the artisan baker, traditional mills are natural partners, as they produce such a range and variety of flours, providing exactly the local quality and distinction that marks them out from "run o' the [roller] mill" bakers. However, getting the best from baking with specialist flours, especially those stoneground from home grown grain, can require a different approach and skills. Marketing and information are important too, as most people do not know very much about the differences between grains, roller and stoneground flours, or artisan baking compared with plant bakeries. English wheat, for example, is generally softer, and tastier than imported wheat, but can produce a dense, less risen loaf. Once people have tasted the difference, they tend to be hooked, and are encouraged to bake their own.

Guild flours can help to give the small artisan baker an edge and a niche in the highly competitive bread market, where very often the only way to compete with the low cost, high volume supermarket offers is to concentrate on something different and special. Some Guild mills have associated bakeries and offer guidance or even courses in traditional bread making using their flours, and many supply small and specialist artisan bakeries. They are developing closer links with local farmers, some of whom are looking to grow specialist, heritage and rare varieties of grains. Think of flours and breads like wine. Just as every vintage, every vintner, and every vineyard has a distinctive quality, so too different mills produce different flours! The Guild encourages you to seek out, visit and support your local traditional mill.

www.tcmg.org.uk

Notes on Real Bread recipes and methods

What loaves should I bake?

Importantly, you need to do your research to find out what your local market demands and take heed of the results. Yes, you can (and arguably should) share with your local community the joys of breads that perhaps they aren't used to buying, but you have to strike the right balance between what you want to bake and what will sell. There's no use in continuing to bake a batch of your favourite 100% sourdough rye every day if nobody's buying it.

The needs of different local markets vary and ultimately it's up to you what you bake but if the majority of your customers are asking for a white tin loaf, the continuation of your business might depend upon you meeting that demand. If so, take pride in baking the best white tin loaf of Real Bread you can and satisfy your personal needs by baking other loaves as specials, which might mean a 3kg batch of dough on a Saturday.

The consensus on how many different breads to bake seems to be: a few types, all made well. This is especially applicable to new bakeries and those with smaller output.

Some suggestions from Colin Hilder:

- Start with a small selection of good quality products and get those into the market – you need the exposure and cash flow.
- Research comparable producers nationally matching your profile and learn from their websites and offerings.
- Research your local competition and market outlets – visit them and talk to them where feasible.
- Don't forget that your business will grow and prosper based on the purchasing habits of conservative shoppers.
- Introduce relevant new products gradually, but be careful not to spend disproportionate amount of time in the test kitchen.
- Try and spot developing national buying trends (examples over the past couple of decades - organic, sourdoughs, ciabatta, spelt, continental breakfast pastries, gluten-free).
- Encourage feedback from your own customers and learn from this – but don't let them dictate your production or distribution by accommodating one-off special requests or special arrangements.
- When ready, add complementary baked or other products with higher margins e.g. cakes, pastries, biscuits and sandwiches. This will increase the order value from the customer, and get extra use (therefore value) out of the oven as the temperature falls after baking bread, and from your other equipment.

If you are intending to start a subscription service then we would advise offering no more than two or three types of loaf at any one time. We started our service offering seven types of bread each week including two rotating specials. While this was great for customers it was a nightmare for us as we had to deal with lots of micro orders each week - sometimes only one person chose a type of bread, so we had to make a single loaf just for them. By limiting the choice you keep your batch sizes up and your administration down. As long as your bread is bloody good then most people are very happy with that limited range.

Because we do subscriptions, retail (two markets per week) and wholesale we now offer eleven types of loaf per week, although not all loaves are available every day, one being a rotating special. During the summer these are: malted and seeded granary, two types of white loaf, baguettes on Saturday, pagnotta (rustic aerated Italian loaf), seeded spelt (Tuesday, Friday and Saturday), sisu 100% rye sourdough (Thursday, Friday and Saturday), pain de campagne, Yorkshire leaven (wheat sourdough made with Yorkshire organic millers flour), sunflower and honey loaf (Thursday and Saturday) plus a weekly special.

Dan McTiernan

Perhaps have a few staples and some changing lines. Start by covering the basics: white, wholemeal, granary. Build up the range slowly. It can be you bake the best bread in the world but that's no use if no one buys it, so you must listen to what people want.

Troels Bendix

Keep it really simple. We started with two choices, and seven months on still only do three - white sourdough, granary sourdough, and 100% rye. Consistency is more important than range. Add in an occasional 'special', if necessary.

Tom Baker

I started with a basic white/wholemeal recipe, one for ordinary bread, one with sourdough, then made it up from there - adding ingredients, substituting amounts - and kept making the ones that sold.

Feline Charpentier

At one point, I was trying out seven or eight different loaves at a time but Carl [Shavitz, Ben's tutor at The School of Artisan Food] advised me to stop, get one 100% right, and perhaps then move on to another.

Ben MacKinnon

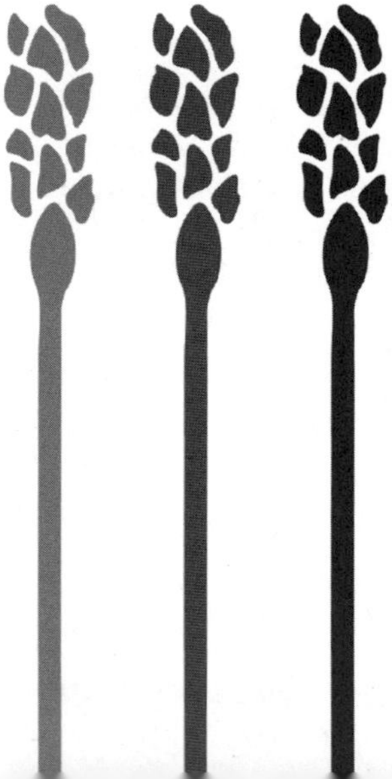

Bakers' percentages

Professional baking recipes (also known as formulae) often work on or include percentages. Perhaps confusingly, this is not a percentage of the total weight of all of the ingredients, but a percentage relative to the weight of flour used, e.g.

1000g flour = 100%
700g water = 70%
20g fresh yeast = 2%
12g salt = 1.2%

As it is based on the total amount of flour, if using more than one type, the percentages would be split between them, e.g.

500g wholemeal flour = 50%
500g rye flour = 50%
750g water = 75%
20g fresh yeast = 2%
1.2g salt = 1.2%

Hydration

This is also based on the ratio of water to flour, so in the above recipes, the dough is said to be at 75% hydration.

Temperature

Home bakers rarely really need to consider temperature control but the larger and more precisely scheduled a bakery gets, the more important it becomes. In the professional bakery, a batch of dough must be ready to bake at the time the oven is available – loaves ready too soon can cause a backlog and over-proved dough, whilst loaves not ready soon enough will result in under-proved dough or an empty oven, which is a waste of time, energy and money.

Assuming the room temperature is around 22-27°C, the dough temperature for a yeasted bread usually should be around 27°C. The easiest way to arrive at this is by taking the temperature of the flour and adjusting the water temperature accordingly. The formula to use is:

(2 x 27) – *ft* = *wt*, where *ft* is the temperature of the flour and *wt* that of the water.

So, if the flour is 20°C then: 2 x 27 = 54 and
54 – 20 = 34 i.e. the water needs to be at 34°C

Other factors to be taken into consideration for larger scale production include ambient temperature, frictional heat generated by mechanical mixing and the temperature of other ingredients, such as the yeast, any preferments, fat and other liquids.

For information on taking into account more variables, see:

www.wildyeastblog.com/2007/07/05/water/
www.starreveld.com/Baking/index.html

Some bakers will always use a thermometer for all measurements, whereas others rely upon the knowledge and experience.

In sourdough, temperature not only has a bearing on proving time but also on the activity of the yeasts and bacteria and therefore the acidity and flavour of the bread. See *Sourdough temperature* on page 40 for more.

Proving, rising or fermentation?

In Britain, the periods during which dough is left to allow the yeast to work are known by several names. It seems that there is no set rule and different bakers have their own preferences as to which period should be called a proof, fermentation or rising. In France, there are three distinct terms: *le pointage* is the time between mixing and dividing/

scaling; and the period from shaping/moulding to baking is *l'apprêt*. In some cases, the dough might be pre-shaped, left to relax for anything up to an hour, and then shaped again. This intermediate period or relaxation is called *la détente*.

Retarding

This is slowing fermentation by keeping the temperature lower than the optimum. In a professional bakery, this is often done in a retarder, but a homebakery may use a fridge or very cool room. The longer proving time caused by retardation allows for extra flavour development and has an effect on other characteristics of the bread. It also gives the baker control over when the dough is ready to be baked – for example, splitting the process between two day shifts, rather than having to work overnight.

Scaling

This is the common bakery term for weighing dough. Dough should always be scaled not only to ensure even baking but also to ensure the finished loaf ends up being the weight you say it is. Dough loses weight through evaporation as it bakes and as a guide, the dough for a standard small (400g) loaf should be scaled at 470g-480g and at 920g-950g for a large (800g) loaf. See the note in the *I fought the law...* chapter on non-standard loaf weights.

Moulding

Moulding or shaping is the process of manipulating the dough to build up tension in its outer surface that will help control the rising and result in the finished loaf having the desired form. The best way to learn is by working alongside an experienced baker, so that you can watch the actions in 3D, copy them and to feel what the dough is doing. He or she will also be able to put you straight if you've not quite got it right.

Without having a baker to hand, then the second best option is watching video clips to see the different techniques bakers use for different loaf shapes. Ask your internet search engine for help on this, using terms such as 'bread shaping,' 'loaf shaping,' or the word 'shaping' paired with the type of loaf you are trying to make.

Dough by Richard Bertinet contains pictures and descriptions of shaping a variety of different loaves and includes a DVD, which demonstrates the techniques.

Tom Herbert has posted a free excerpt from his online bread making download videos clip, which showing how to shape a tin loaf, at:

www.youtube.com/user/ThomasHugoHerbert#p/a/u/2/vzwv_BErOH0

See the links chapter at the back of this guide for links to some more free online bread shaping video clips.

Baking times

Recipes will advise baking times but if making adjustments to the recipe, scaling or method given, you need to bear in mind that you might also have to adjust the baking time and/or temperature.

Baking times will depend on the weight and type of product and the oven temperature. If an 800g tin loaf baked at 230°C takes around 30 minutes, then a 400g loaf might take 22-25 minutes and rolls (e.g. 100g) 15-18 minutes. An enriched dough will require a lower oven temperature as sugars, fruit, butter, milk and some other ingredients colour and burn easily.

Shape will also affect baking time. For example, even if a baguette weighs 400g, its high surface area to volume ratio would mean the baking time would be the same as (or perhaps less than) that of a 100g roll.

Basic methods of bread making

Andrew Whitley outlines the small number of basic categories into which bread making techniques around the world fall.

Straight yeasted dough

All the flour, yeast, water and salt (plus any other ingredients) are mixed together, fermented in bulk for a period of time, divided, proved and baked. As outlined above, the process can be retarded by reducing temperature.

Sponge-and-dough

A pre-ferment (known variously as a sponge, biga or poolish) consisting of a portion of the flour and water plus all the (manufactured) yeast is fermented for a number of hours (often overnight) before being mixed with the remaining flour and water, plus the salt and other additions such as fat. Such doughs can be started with very small amounts of manufactured yeast because there is time during the sponge stage for it to multiply. Organic acids form in the sponge and have a gluten strengthening effect on the final dough, as well as contributing fuller flavour.

Old dough (also known as *pâte fermentée*), a portion of a previous day's bread dough, is different from other pre-ferments in that it will include any other ingredients that might have been in the dough - anything from salt to malted grains or even nuts or seeds. Old dough contributes extra flavour and a certain amount of gluten strengthening due to the acids that have formed since the 'old' dough was first mixed.

However, old dough cannot easily be used by itself like other (flour, water and yeast) pre-ferments, i.e. to initiate a larger sponge or dough, because the presence of salt and other ingredients may have interfered with the balance of yeasts and bacteria. It's not impossible, but it isn't nearly as neat as using a simple (yeast, flour and water) pre-ferment. For this reason, some bakers do not class old dough as a pre-ferment.

Sourdough or leaven

Naturally-occurring yeasts and bacteria, present in the flour, ferment and multiply to form a stable culture that produces enough gas to aerate bread dough and significant quantities of acids which act on the gluten structure, as well as contributing the characteristic 'tangy' flavour of this type of bread. After the formation of an initial starter which may take 3-5 days, sourdough systems usually involve three stages:

1. The starter is 'refreshed' by adding more than its weight in new flour and water.

2. The refreshed starter is fermented, typically for 12-24 hours, to make a production starter.

3. Most of the production starter is used to make the final dough. The remainder is conserved to become the starter for the next batch of bread.

The final dough in sourdough systems has anywhere from 20-60% sourdough starter in it, reflecting the relative lack of yeast concentration compared with straight or sponge-and-dough systems that use highly-concentrated manufactured yeast. Proof times are therefore considerably extended for sourdough breads.

Enriched doughs

These have extra ingredients added – such as sugar, oil, nuts, seeds, fruits, herbs and spices – at levels that significantly alter the dough structure and behaviour, as well as the eating experience. Enriched doughs may be raised with either manufactured yeast or sourdough. They require special handling during the mixing and moulding of the dough and at the baking stage.

Laminated doughs

Layers of hard fat (e.g. butter, lard or margarine) are folded between layers of dough so that both the expansion of the fat during baking and the aeration provided by the yeast in the dough contribute to creating a very open and flaky texture. Typical examples are croissants and Danish pastries.

Your starter for ten

Andrew Whitley on starting and maintaining a sourdough culture.

The word leaven is often used to denote natural fermentations of wheat (without bakers' yeast), with sourdough often being used for rye and other cereals. But this is not a hard distinction and the word sourdough is generally understood to cover long fermentations of any flour without baker's yeast in which naturally-occurring yeasts and bacteria proliferate.

Starting a starter

There is no need to use anything other than flour and water to start a leaven or sourdough. Recipes that involve ingredients such as grapes, apple skins and yoghurt are based on a misunderstanding of the science of sourdough fermentation and should be disregarded.

The surface of grains, such as wheat and rye, are usually home to thriving colonies of one or more types of yeast and bacteria. These live in symbiotic relationship with the grain and so are, arguably, the most suitable to start a sourdough culture. Other ingredients are therefore unnecessary but here are some that might be suggested, along with some theories behind their inclusion:

- *Rhubarb. Acids can help deter pathogenic (bad) micro organisms and create an environment favoured by lactic acid bacteria.*
- *Hops also have anti-bacterial properties.*
- *Live yoghurt is also acidic and contains lactic acid bacteria, though not necessarily the types most suitable for producing bread.*
- *Mashed potato provides an extra source of food for yeast and bacteria.*
- *Grapes, raisins, sultanas and so on have yeasts and bacteria on their skins but again, not necessarily the types most suited to making bread.*
- *Honey is high in sugars, on which the yeast can feed. Unpasteurised honey might also contain yeasts and bacteria.*

Sourdough temperature

As well as one or more types of yeast, sourdough cultures contain Lactobacilli (lactic acid bacteria) that produce both lactic and acetic acids. A key part of mastering sourdough is keeping the concentration and ratio of these acids in balance. Too much acetic acid and the bread will taste very sharp and perhaps vinegary (it is the same acid that is found in vinegar), whereas bread with too little acetic acid and a higher level of lactic acid might not have any discernible sourdough characteristics.

Different yeasts and bacteria are adapted to different conditions. Lactobacilli that produce higher levels of lactic acid tend to prefer wetter batters kept at around 1-5°C, whilst those producing both lactic and acetic acid thrive better in stiffer batters kept at around 20°C. Acetic acid is produced in lower quantities than lactic and so takes longer to build up in a dough.

Therefore, to achieve a more pronounced flavour and sourness, you can try keeping your starter at a lower hydration (i.e. dough-like) and retard dough fermentation by proving overnight in the fridge. For a milder flavour and acidity, try keeping your starter as a batter and prove at room temperature.

See the Bookshelf chapter for publications, websites and courses that look at sourdough in depth. You can find (and join in with) many discussions about sourdough at:

http://sourdough.com/forum

Feeding

Once a sourdough starter is initiated (see the four-day process detailed below), it should be stable - in the sense that it raises bread reliably and produces the same flavour whenever it is used, subject to any marked changes in the ingredients with which it is mixed.

There is no need to 'feed' a starter during prolonged periods between uses. It is a waste of time and can lead to an unnecessary build up of starter, which then cannot all be used. When planning a batch of sourdough bread, remove your starter from the fridge, refresh it according to the instructions below (or pro rata depending on how much bread you are going to make) and leave it to ferment for the requisite period. The function of refreshment is:

- To dilute the starter in a much larger body of fresh flour and water, reducing any excessive acidity that has built up.
- To provide a new source of sugars and other resources for the existing yeasts and bacteria to metabolise.
- To introduce new yeasts and bacteria into the sourdough from the fresh flour.

Storing a sourdough between uses

If you are using a sourdough daily, it can be safely left at ambient temperature between uses, except in very hot weather when it may become over-ripe if it is allowed to go above 40°C. Over-ripeness results in an excessive production of organic acids (such as lactic and acetic acids) and a diminution of yeast activity due to the exhaustion of fermentable sugars in the dough and higher levels of acid inhibiting their metabolism. Using an over-ripe sourdough is possible, but needs care. The best way of reducing its effect is to reduce (e.g. by half) the amount of starter in the refreshment stage, thus further diluting the effect of the existing organisms and their by-products.

If the starter is likely to be used less frequently than daily it should be stored in a fridge at 5°C. Take care to keep it in a plastic container with a close-fitting lid. Don't use glass jars with metal clip seals: glass should be avoided in the bakery anyway and considerable pressure can build up in the sourdough pot, so the 'safety valve' of a plastic lid seal is useful. Take care to avoid cross-contamination from potential sources of mould that might infect the 'scum' around the inside of the top of a sourdough tub and thence the main body of sourdough.

Long-term storage

For periods longer than four weeks, a sensible strategy is to keep the starter in the freezer. In this state, biological decay slows down to almost zero and the sourdough will hardly change while frozen. Some of the yeasts may be damaged by freezing, so an additional interim refreshment may be called for to bring a frozen sourdough up to full vigour.

Too much sourdough starter

A build-up of unused sourdough starter sometimes happens. This very acid material can be used, at ratios of 5% or less, to enhance almost any other dough, apart from those where even a hint of sourness or discolouration would be unacceptable. Just add the old sourdough at dough mixing time along with the other ingredients.

Some basic Real Bread recipes

As there are hundreds of books and websites crammed with recipes already out there (some of which are listed in the *Bookshelf* chapter), we're just going to give you a few basics.

The number of loaves each will produce depends on whether you scale at 400g, 800g or as small rolls.

8 hour yeasted straight white bread

Peter Cook

31.75kg strong white flour
17kg water
113.5g yeast
510g salt*
113.5g shortening

Makes around 50 large loaves

We mix three minutes on slow and eight minutes on fast as our mixer only has two speeds. The dough has 7-8 hours bulk fermentation, then it is cut out of the trough, scaled, moulded into whatever shape then proved. This is in the ambient temperature of the bakery and the length of proof depends on what kind of bread it will be, and what the temperature/time of year is. A sandwich loaf takes about 90 minutes, but a tin loaf, which has to rise further would be about 140 minutes. Baking is 35-45 minutes at 230-240°C, depending on loaf size.

** you would need to reduce this to meet the Food Standards Agency's 1% target.*

Straight yeasted wholemeal bread

Andrew Whitley

5kg 100% wholemeal flour
3.5kg water
80g fresh yeast
60g salt
150g olive oil or butter
900g old dough (optional)

Makes 10 large loaves

Mix and work to form a smooth and slightly elastic dough. Leave to ferment for at least two hours, (preferably 3-4 hours) at 25°C. Fold the dough over on itself, scale and shape as desired. Bake at 230°C, turning the oven down to 200°C after the first 10 minutes. The remaining baking time will be about 30 minutes for large loaves.

24 hour sponge

In this recipe, Paul Barker includes bakers' percentages

1000g Bread flour = 100%
10g Fresh yeast = 1%
15g Salt = 1.5%
50g Starter* = 5%
500g Water = 50%
Total = 1575 g

**optional. Cinnamon Square's starter – the CS Sour – is rye, kept at 50-60% hydration.*

Mix all the ingredients together to make a smooth dough, and leave covered for 18-24 hours in a cool (15-20°C), dry room.

Wholemeal bread (sponge and dough method)

Paul Barker's recipe using the above 24 hour sponge at 40% of flour weight

2000g Wholemeal flour = 100%
800g Wholemeal sponge = 40%
36g Salt = 1.8%
40g White shortening = 2%
40g Yeast = 2%
1300g Water = 65%
Total = 4216g

Mix all the ingredients together to form a smooth dough. Scale into desired weights, and leave to prove for 30 minutes. Shape as desired and bake at 230ºC for around 30-40 minutes for large loaves.

Wheat sourdough starter/ leaven

Andrew Whitley

Day 1

350g	flour (wholemeal)
250g	warm water (at 30°C)
600g	**total**

Mix the flour and water together, cover and ferment at as close to 30°C as possible for 24 hours.

Day 2

600g	starter from day 1
350g	flour (wholemeal)
250g	warm water (30°C)
1200g	**total**

Again, mix all ingredients together and ferment for 24 hours.

Day 3

1200g	starter from day 2
350g	flour (wholemeal)
250g	warm water (30° C)
1800g	**total**

Method as before.

Day 4

1800g	starter from Day 3
600g	white flour
150g	wholemeal flour
450g	warm water (30° C)
2950g	**total (original leaven)**

Method as before. After 24 hours, you can use some of this original leaven (sometimes called starter) to make a production leaven and bread, as in the following recipe.

White sourdough bread

Stage 1 - refreshing the leaven/starter

1200g	water
2000g	flour (75/25 white/wholemeal or as you prefer)
1600g	original leaven
4800g	**total (production leaven)**

Ferment for four hours at ambient (20-25°C) or for 12 hours at 8-12°C. Then use this production leaven to make your dough.

Stage 2 - final dough

3000g	refreshed production leaven (the rest becomes or adds to your pot of original leaven)
4000g	flour (75/25 white/wholemeal or as you prefer)
3000g	water
80g	salt
10.08kg	**total**

Mix to a dough, preferably adding the production leaven towards the end of mixing. Divide, mould and place in proving baskets or couches. Proof will usually take 4-5 hours under a rack cover with no added heat. Bake at 220ºC for around 30-40 minutes for large loaves.

Rye sourdough starter

Andrew Whitley

Day 1

250g	wholemeal rye flour (not light rye flour)
500g	warm water (30°C)
750g	total

Mix, cover and ferment at as close to 30°C as possible for 24 hours.

Day 2

750g	starter from day 1
250g	wholemeal rye flour
500g	warm water (at 30°C)
1500g	**total**

Method as above.

Day 3

1500g	starter from day 2
250g	wholemeal rye flour
500g	warm water (at 30°C)
2250g	**total**

Ferment for 24 hours.

Day 4

2250g	starter from day 3
300g	wholemeal rye flour
400g	warm water (at 30°C)
3000g	**total (sourdough starter)**

Method as above. Thereafter, use some or all of this sourdough starter to make a production sourdough and bread as in the following recipe.

100% sourdough rye bread

Stage 1 - production sourdough

500g	sourdough starter
1500g	wholemeal rye flour
3000g	water
5000g	**total production sourdough**

Mix together, cover and ferment for 12-24 hours at warm ambient temperature (25-30°C). Then use this sourdough to make your dough.

Stage 2 - final dough

4500g	refreshed production sourdough (the rest becomes or adds to your pot of sourdough starter)
3400g	rye flour (wholemeal or light as you prefer)
2100g	water
50g	salt
10.05kg	**total**

Mix together to form a very sloppy dough. Scale (as a guide, try 930g for an 800g loaf and 480g for a 400g one) and scoop the dough into greased tins to prove. If the tin was half full when you start, then the dough will be ready when it has almost reached the top. Proof could take anything from 2-8 hours, depending on the vigour of your starter and the ambient temperature – this is something that you will just have to learn by experience of baking with your own starter in your own bakehouse.

Bake at 240ºC for 10 minutes and then reduce to 220ºC. Continue baking for a further 40-50 minutes (large loaves) or 25-35 minutes (small loaves).

As this loaf is very sticky and difficult to slice immediately after baking, it can (and perhaps should) be sold the day after baking. The natural preservative and anti-staling effect of the lactic acid bacteria in the starter means that the loaf will remain in edible for perhaps a week.

Enriched bread (sponge and dough method)

Andrew Whitley

This can be used to make a fruited loaf or buns. It is easily adapted by omitting the fruit and nuts or by adding one or more ground 'sweet' spices, such as cinnamon, clove, cardamom and allspice.

Sponge

1300g	strong bread flour (white, wholemeal or a mixture)
40g	fresh yeast
950g	warm water (at 30°C)
2290g	**total sponge**

Mix, cover and ferment at ambient temperature for 12-20 hours.

Final dough

2250g	overnight sponge
1700g	flour (white, wholemeal or a mixture)
750g	butter
550g	sugar (preferably raw cane)
750g	egg
4kg	mixed dried fruits and nuts
10kg	**total**

Mix everything except the fruit/nut mix to a soft dough. Fold in the fruits and nuts until evenly distributed, taking care not to over mix, which will pulp the fruit. Ferment in bulk for two hours. Divide, mould and prove. Bake in a moderate (approx 180ºC) oven to prevent burning. Small loaves will take around 30-40 minutes.

Note: the mixed fruits and nuts are best soaked overnight in water, fruit juice or an alcoholic drink, like rum or brandy. Any liquid that has not been absorbed overnight may be used to replace an equal amount of the water when making the final dough.

Laminated dough (for croissants and pains au chocolat)

Andrew Whitley

Dough

2400g	strong white flour
30g	salt
70g	fresh yeast
1500g	scalded milk (i.e. heated to 80°C then cooled to 5-8°C)
4000g	**total**

To laminate

1000g butter (refrigerated)

Mix first four ingredients together and work to form dough of fairly firm consistency. Chill to 10°C.

Pin dough to a rectangle about 10mm thick. Pin out the butter to cover two-thirds of the dough. Fold in three, pin out and fold in three again (i.e. one half turn). Return to the chiller for minimum 30-90 minutes.

Pin out a little longer than before and give a 'book turn', i.e. folding the edges to the middle and the same again. Return to the chiller for 30-90 minutes. Following this pattern of turns should produce 24 layers of butter between the layers of dough.

Finally pin out to about 4mm thick and cut out right-angled triangles for croissants or rectangles for pain au chocolat. Roll up, glaze with egg, prove and bake at 200ºC for 15 minutes.

KENNY'S
FRESH BAKED
BREAD
FOCACCIA
£3.5
CIABATTA
£3.5
SOURDOUG

Different types of Real Bread bakeries and outlets

What legal structure do you want the bakery to have? You will only be eligible for grants if you are a non-profit making organisation, such as a community group or a social enterprise. Getting a grant at the beginning means that you are determining the long-term financial make up of your organisation. Maybe you like the idea of the benefiting personally from the profits? In which case look for a loan or private investors, rather than grants.

For free advice on local food structures visit Making Local Food Work: www.mlfw.co.uk/training

Different business models

Sole Trader

This is defined as a business set up and run by one individual owner. Many food businesses that operate from home have sole trader status. This is by far the least complicated and most common type of business. However, you should be aware of the liability that this status has for the owner. It means that you:

- Have total control, but also responsibility over all aspects of your business.
- Make all the decisions regarding investment, funding and products.
- Receive any financial surplus as profit.
- Are personally responsible for any business debt incurred and any liabilities.
- Are required to pay your own National Insurance contributions.
- Are taxed on the profit of your business as personal income.

Partnership

This is defined as two or more people trading together as a single business entity. If you decide to run your business with another person such as a friend or spouse, your business will operate with partnership status. This means that:

- A formal partnership agreement covering the responsibilities and rights of each partner should be drawn up by a solicitor. This can also provide details of how the profits will be shared.
- Partners usually share the responsibility for running the business.
- You will be liable for your own and your partner's business debts.
- Each partner pays their own National Insurance contributions and income tax on their share of any profit.
- You do not need to register your business name.

Other types

- Private limited company – Is registered as such at Companies House and has one or more shareholders.
- Franchise – A company/operator is licensed to trade as a given brand or using a particular name. The brand owner will usually provide training, supply chain, business model and other support for the franchisee.
- Co-operative – the International Co-operative Alliance defines a co-operative as 'an autonomous association of persons united voluntarily to meet their common economic, social, and cultural needs and aspirations through a jointly-owned and democratically-controlled enterprise.'[7]
- Social enterprise – "...a business with primarily social objectives whose surpluses are principally reinvested for that purpose in the business or in the community, rather than being driven by the need to maximise profits for shareholders and owners".[8]

Any business has a number of essential components. The first three are:

- *Technical/production skill or input.*
- *Sales/marketing skill or input.*
- *Administrative/financial skill or input.*

Which do you have and, more importantly, which do you not have and where is it going to come from? The fourth component is sufficient finance for capital investment and trading costs. When calculating your figures, my rule of thumb is to add 50% to the figure you first thought of, or look at the effect of your sales projections dipping by 25% to 50%.

Colin Hilder

Outlets

These are some of the main alternatives to selling direct from a high street bakery.

Stalls

A stall at a farmers', community or other local market can offer added value (e.g. sandwiches and other ready to eat products) and volume of sales but they involve a lot of work in terms of supplying, setting up and staffing. As well as the costs involved in these, demand can be unpredictable, potentially leading to the cost of waste disposal, selling discounted loaves below the cost of production or simply throwing or giving loaves away.

If access to good food is a key concern you've identified and want to address, you might be able to run a stall on a temporary basis at a place convenient for those who you want to benefit from being able to buy Real Bread. This might be in or just outside a community centre, a school or a church hall.

Remember, unless you are operating the stall on private land, you will need a street trading licence. See the *I fought the law* chapter for more.

See below for a list of local market organisations, several of which offer a range of advice and support for their members and stallholders.

- National Association of Farmers Markets
  www.farmersmarkets.net
- Country Markets
  www.country-markets.co.uk
- London Farmers' Markets
  www.lfm.org.uk
- Farmers' Markets in Wales
  www.fmiw.co.uk
- Scottish Farmers' Markets
  www.scottishfarmersmarkets.co.uk

Deliveries

Delivery allows you to increase your market by reaching out to customers who can't or won't make the journey to your bakery. Your rounds might be daily or only one or two times a week, depending on demand and your bakery's capacity. Downsides of delivery include staff time and cost; costs of buying or renting, maintaining and running a vehicle, as well as the negative environmental impacts if that vehicle runs on fossil fuel.

Ben McKinnon of the E5 Bakehouse in Hackney delivers to his regular customers using a bicycle trailer. Similarly, Tom Baker of Loaf in the suburbs of Birmingham loads his loaves into panniers on his bike, though if the weather's bad he does the weekly drop offs on the number 11 bus.

The Thoughtful Bread Company uses a van fuelled by recycled cooking oil biodiesel, filled using a solar-powered pump.

AJ Jones of Hay on Wye has an arrangement with the community shop, Hopes of Longtown, who meet the van halfway, where someone from the shop also picks up its meat and pies supply.

We have a drop-off twice per week at two local real ale pubs for subscribers. We also deliver twice per week to a market seven miles away and to Manchester, which involves three deliveries. Otherwise we try to encourage customers to collect from us.

Dan McTiernan

Bread van

Falling somewhere between a stall and delivery is a bread van is a mobile shop, which you can park at different locations on given set days or half days. This is an option if you want to reach out to people right around your local area, perhaps because there are several urban estates or rural villages that are Real Bread deserts, i.e. with no bakery or other place to buy a loaf within walking distance.

Although this has the negative environmental impact of running a vehicle, it might be lower than that of each of your customers driving to you. Perhaps you could team up with another local producer or food co-operative to increase the range (and appeal) of your offering and help share costs.

You will need a street trading licence for a bread van.

Food hub

This is a modified delivery system, where a group of customers clubs together to place a single collective order, allowing the baker to take a single payment and drop off at an agreed point and time. See the *Community Supported Baking* chapter for more on this.

My outlet here in my home village, a café, is run by people who are totally committed to the concept of local food; leaving aside the issue of raw materials, pretty much everything they sell is made within nine miles of here: in my case, about nine yards.

Steve Rickaby

Through a food co-operative or local community enterprise

Supplying (or setting up as) a local community owned or operated food enterprise is a great way of putting Real Bread at the heart of that group. It also gets Real Bread to those who may otherwise have difficulty with access to healthy, real food, whether that's because of restrictions on mobility, personal finance, or proximity to supply. For more see www.sustainweb.org/realbread/on_the_menu/

We supply 60-80 loaves once a week to our local veg box scheme. They drop about 20 boxes here when they pick up the bread, which their customers then come and collect. Because this has been happening for years, and we have an excellent relationship with them, we give them a special price on the bread, lower than our standard wholesale prices. We charge them £1.00 or £1.20 for each 400g loaf, depending on the type of loaf.

The benefits are many - it gets our bread delivered out to people who don't live close enough to come to us and buy it, through the packaging people find out about our charity and its work, the scheme promotes events for us via fliers in the boxes, we get business from them when they have barbeques and open days and sometimes we get vegetables at cost price. As we make the bread for the events, our charity gets a regular income and our co-workers (patients) learn a little about working for a business.

John Forrester

A mixed operation

You might find that the adage 'man cannot live by bread alone' applies to your situation and that you need to diversify what you offer, either by producing a wider range, buying in products to sell on, or teaming up with other producers selling a variety of products from one shared outlet – e.g. a co-operatively owned shop.

We have small café area, so we do have a bit of everything. As well as the bakery, my partner makes fresh pasties, quiches, and salads, and we sell general groceries. There just isn't enough of a profit margin in bread alone in our situation and without the deli part of the business, we would not have survived. In the small rural town in which we are based we just can't charge a premium for an artisan product - we simply wouldn't have kept the customers - the only other bakery in town (a chain) just closed down this week!! As to costing, I work on the basis of a third for the cost of making it, a third to make it and a third for profit - roughly anyway! Quite often it comes down to what you would pay for the product yourself, and whether you can afford to sell it at that price.

Feline Charpentier

A greengrocer's shop was being sold in Slaithwaite. The community wanted to rescue it, so issued shares and bought it. They invited us to collaborate, which was great because both businesses have a very similar ethos, we are able to share the premises and therefore costs and provide a fabulous shop for people that sells fresh fruit and veg (local as much as possible), fish, dairy, whole foods and Real Bread that you can see being made at the back of the shop.

Dan McTiernan

Wholesale

An alternative (or addition) to selling direct to members of the public is supplying retailers or food businesses, such as cafés and restaurants.

Here are some thoughts from Colin Hilder on supplying retailers:

- Decide if you are concentrating on retailers or selling direct through street/farm markets.
- Good retailers understand their consumer base, can make sensible buying decisions, will market your products and are responsible for waste.
- Look for opportunities with local delis, restaurants, pubs and caterers.
- Don't get into sale or return unless you are keen to store old mouldy products, or are feeding pigs and ducks.
- Whatever medium you use for your catalogue and order sheet, make ordering easy for the retailer. Give clear product information with description, ingredients, photographs and a clear list with prices and codes for ordering. Send a fresh list out regularly - at least monthly and perhaps weekly.
- Set up a website and let it do the work and save you from many lengthy phone calls and mailings. It only needs to be basic at first but with good quality photos and clear, concise information. You can then develop it as the business grows.
- Distribution costs are potentially deadly for a wholesale business, so try for business from customers geographically close to you at first and then, when you are ready, grow the radius gradually.
- Secure at least one retail outlet with a regular substantial order to act as your core outlet and to test your new ideas.
- Don't go for cheap, half-dead vans for distribution – they will break down at 4am as the delivery run starts, may be off the road for servicing more often than on it, the servicing costs will be very high and the drivers will hate them.
- Do not use short-term hire or short-term lease vehicles. Look for new or low mileage vans on long rental terms (drive them for 10,000 miles and exchange for a newish replacement - no servicing costs) or on lease with deferred residual payment at end of term. Why? Good vans, happy drivers, impressed customers, low service costs and so GOOD CASHFLOW!
- Don't permit drivers to contravene parking, congestion charges or other traffic regulations. If a penalty does come through, pay it immediately to avoid tear-making default costs or, worse still, bailiff costs - they can double your distribution costs. Consider including in the driver's contract that after a given point (e.g. verbal warning for the first incidence, written warning for a second) payment of such fines will be deducted from his or her wages.
- Get loaded and started really early in the morning. If delivering in central London, get in and out before 7am, after which the Congestion Charge will apply and traffic will be very slow moving.
- Use a satnav to set up and optimise your journey routings. You may know the route like the back of your hand but the relief or emergency driver might not and some don't know north from west!
- Wait until you are ready before supplying supermarkets. In my experience, I feel that they can have rigid rules on delivery schedules, payment terms, discounts and sometimes might try to extract a large non-returnable payment up-front for the privilege of trying your products in an outlet, before dumping you if sales fail to meet target within a few weeks.
- Be prepared for a non-social life with lots of midnight phone calls but be proud to be making an effort to provide excellence and offer a *real* alternative to junk dietary habits.

Community Supported Baking

In November 2009, LandShare Community Interest Company organised the Rise of Real Bread conference to mark the first anniversaries of the Oxford Bread Group and the Real Bread Campaign. A workshop on Community Supported Baking (CSB) was scheduled for the lunch break but despite this having been advertised long in advance, only a handful of the 150 conference delegates signed up to attend. This all changed following a presentation by two pioneers of CSB in the UK, Dan and Johanna McTiernan of The Handmade Bakery, which generated such interest that we were forced to turn delegates away from the workshop's overcrowded venue.

What is Community Supported Baking?

Long-championed by Real Bread Campaign co-founder, Andrew Whitley of Bread Matters, the inspiration for Community Supported Baking (CSB) for comes from Community Supported Agriculture (CSA). The Soil Association describes this as "a partnership between farmers and consumers where, at best, the responsibilities and rewards of farming are shared."

The current consensus amongst those in the UK who are part of what rapidly is becoming a movement is that a CSB is not simply a bakery serving a local community, but one where the risks and rewards of baking are shared. A CSB might take the form of a workers' co-operative or social enterprise but whatever its set up, it should blur the traditional 'me baker / you customer' line, with members of the community becoming what the Slow Food movement calls 'co-producers'.

For more information on CSA, visit:

www.makinglocalfoodwork.co.uk/about/csa/index.cfm
www.soilassociation.org/Takeaction/Getinvolvedlocally/Communitysupportedagriculture/tabid/201/Default.aspx

Why set up a Community Supported Bakery?

Potential benefits for the baker:

- Help from local people to set up a new bakery.
- Working capital.
- More secure and predictable cash flow.
- Local labour.
- Less food waste.
- Enhanced social engagement - a greater sense of place and belonging in a community.
- Practical help e.g. with distribution.

Running the CSB has really helped me put roots down in my adopted local community, I know all my customers by their first names, and often their children and pets too!

Tom Baker

Potential benefits for the consumer:

- Greater connection to where your bread comes from.
- Learning about baking.
- Community development.
- A lower price for exceptional quality bread.
- Fair trade - a fair price to the baker, the consumer and perhaps even back through the chain to the producers and suppliers of basic ingredients.
- A financial stake in an ethical enterprise.
- Convenience of having bread delivered to, or being available at, a hub that's more accessible than the bakery.

Sometimes it feels almost like we're providing therapy in a warm paper bag, that's how happy it seems to make some of our customers.

Dan McTiernan

CSB models

There are many different possible configurations for partnerships between bakery and community. The most suitable in your situation depends upon what inputs (skills, time, labour, finance, property...) the various involved parties are able and willing to contribute and what outputs (bread, return on investment, training, community space...) they want.

Community ownership

A CSB could be owned and run by its customers. They might rent a bakery and be responsible for employing the bakers and how the enterprise functions. In terms of finance, the group would first agree on the set up and running costs. The group would then agree to how much each member invests (either financially or in kind) in the CSB and how much (and in what form) each will receive in return.

For example, a co-operative with 400 members paying £2 per week each. This covers the running costs of a bakery including wages. In return they each receive a loaf a week and collectively have full control of the bakery that supplies them.

Capital investment

Unless baking from home, setting up a bakery requires a lot of capital. One way for a community to support a bakery is to provide the capital in the form of loans to, or shares in, the business. This might be done in a way that offers reasonable reward or interest to the local investors. Local investors in this way truly share the risks and rewards of baking.

In-kind investments

In-kind investments could include waiving/reducing costs of: property rental, flour, grain, milling, equipment, labour for fitting out the bakery, shifts running the shop, shifts in the bakehouse, another local business adding bread on its own delivery rounds, and helping in 'back office' (accounts, ordering and marketing) support.

Bread bonds

Subscribers making a financial investment in the CSB receive their share dividends, interest payments or even (though less likely) repayment of the loan itself in bread. At the time of writing, The Handmade Bakery was just about to start what is perhaps Britain's first bread bond scheme.

Bread as bread

As local produce hits seasonal gluts, the CSB could offer customers discounts on or payments in bread for those ingredients that could be used in loaves e.g. apples, herbs, potatoes, nuts and berries.

It is less likely that the CSB enters into a permanent alternative payment agreement with local suppliers but perhaps a miller, cheese maker or butcher would accept bread as part payment for ingredients occasionally. See the section on 'alternative' payments in the *Money matters and admin* chapter for some examples.

Subscription schemes

Customers commit to and pay in advance for a certain number of loaves over a given period of time e.g. two loaves per week for three months. As well as helping the CSB with cash flow, it gives a better idea of demand, thereby reducing risk of food waste.

In return, as well as a guaranteed supply of fresh, Real Bread, subscribers receive a discount (perhaps increasing in line with increasing level of commitment) on the CSB's standard single loaf price.

Loaf social enterprise runs a CSB from director Tom Baker's home in Cotteridge, South Birmingham. As well as supplying three retail outlets, Tom has 20 subscribers who pay a monthly subscription of £11 to the bakery and in return have a large loaf of sourdough baked for them each Friday, which they collect from his house every Friday evening. Tom bakes mainly for neighbours in Cotteridge, although a few people come from further afield.

Apprenticeship / volunteering

As with any enterprise, labour is a major cost. Members of the local community could become co-producers in a CSB by providing their time in return for alternative payments e.g. bread, returned favours or an official LETS (Local Exchange Trading System or Scheme).

See www.letslinkuk.net for more.

A more established CSB could enter into a relationship with the wider community of Real Bread bakers by offering an apprenticeship/internship. In this case, the exchange would be the trainee baker giving time in return for the chance to gain skills and experience. See the chapter on *People* for more.

Making volunteering work can be easier said than done. When you are just starting out then any help is always gratefully received. I slipped a disk three weeks into starting to bake... believe me, volunteers saved us at that point and one of them ended up joining us permanently. In fact four of our volunteers are now employed in one way or another by the bakery. We have requests every week now from potential volunteers, which is great in one way, but also starts to become a management issue in itself.

Dan McTiernan

Food hubs and buying co-ops

Food hubs and buying co-operatives operate on a not-for-profit basis and aim to use bulk orders to reduce the price of goods. Both systems can help with getting Real Bread to people who otherwise would have difficulty (e.g. financial, social or geographic) accessing it. A CSB can work in partnership with or even incorporate a food hub or buying co-op.

In common with many small businesses, one of the issues facing local bakeries is steady cash flow. Local people can help by forming a co-operative buying group that regularly purchases a quantity of bread between them. Co-op members arrange individual orders, payments and distribution of bread amongst themselves, so all the bakery has to worry about is a single order, drop off and payment.

Buying hubs are similar but act to sell or distribute food to others. A community owned village shop or a bread stall run by residents of a housing estate that does not have a bakery within walking distance, or even a workplace could act as one.

For everything you ever wanted to know about food hubs and buying co-ops, and probably even more that you didn't know you wanted to know, visit www.foodcoops.org

I use a food co-op to order some of my bulk ingredients from Suma Wholefoods such as salt, seeds, whole grains, so as well as supplying loaves to a food co-op, it can work both ways by helping when you're too small to place your own Suma order.

Tom Baker

Getting the local community involved

Dan McTiernan's advice is:

In short, talk to them! Attend local events and festivals. We did several local events giving out bread tasters and information and conducting surveys (we conducted an online survey using Survey Monkey, www.surveymonkey.com). We also tapped into existing organisations that had mailing lists such as our local Transition Towns initiative. There will be lots of people out there interested in seeing Real Bread in their community and for all kinds of different reasons such as: organics, child nutrition, job creation, community shopping improvement, carbon reduction. Just look around for those already working in areas such as these, and introduce yourself.

Examples

This is a selection of the CSBs in the UK that we know about so far. All have said that they are happy to chat to other people who want to learn more about their stories.

The Handmade Bakery

Slaithwaite, Yorkshire

Not-for-profit bakers Dan and Johanna McTiernan and Matt Betts offer a subscription scheme and are working on setting up bread bonds, in which interest repayments on loans from members of the local community will be repaid in bread. Having started by baking at home and later borrowing the pizza oven of a local Italian restaurant twice a week, they now bake their Real Bread at the back of the community-owned Green Valley Grocer in Slaithwaite, Yorkshire. They are due to expand in 2011.
www.thehandmadebakery.coop

The Hornbeam Centre

Walthamstow, London

The Hornbeam Community provides a kitchen meeting space, computer and printing facilities, use of their account with Suma Wholefoods for ordering ingredients, and covers the costs of some promotional materials without charge to Pilar Lopez, who runs the CSB. In return, Pilar and four other bakers (three of whom bake at home and deliver to the centre by bike or by foot) give their time to bake loaves for the centre's community café and weekly farmers' market at cost price. Pilar's contribution also includes running the centre's bread making classes.
www.hornbeam.org.uk/cafe

Loaf Social Enterprises

Cotteridge, Birmingham

At the time of writing Tom was baking around 50 loaves at a time, the maximum that his space would allow. With 20 subscribers each paying £11 per month for a loaf a week (the extra loaves sold through two local shops), the bakery is only making a profit if labour costs are not taken into account. It is the cookery classes and extra activities (e.g. making pizzas in a mobile oven at events) that make Loaf viable as a full-time business. Tom is working to move to larger premises and purchase equipment (notably a mixer) to allow the bakery part of the business to become self-funding and even generate a surplus to be re-invested in further food access work.
www.loafonline.co.uk

The Oxford Bread Group

Around Oxford (from a bakery in Wheatley)

Cereal breeder, archeobotanist and thatcher John Letts' believes that you cannot call a loaf Real Bread unless it has been made with real flour, which he believes can only be made from heritage or ancient grains, grown in low-input conditions. John works with local farmers to grow mixed populations of ancient and heritage wheats (the sale or other exchange of which frustratingly is illegal under EU and British seed marketing regulations), which produce both good thatching straw and bread making flour. The grain is stoneground and then baked by Geoff Coleman at the Cornfield Bakery to produce The Oxford Loaf. This is distributed to subscribers (minimum 3 month commitment) through 15 food hubs and sold at some restaurants and farmers' markets. The group also sells its heritage flour.
www.oxfordlocalbread.org

We have included a list of considerations to help a group of people decide what it wants from a CSB in *Appendix 1: Community Supported Bakery start up checklist.*

We continue to list more CSBs on our website and if would like to share with others what you've learned in you own, please email realbread@sustainweb.org

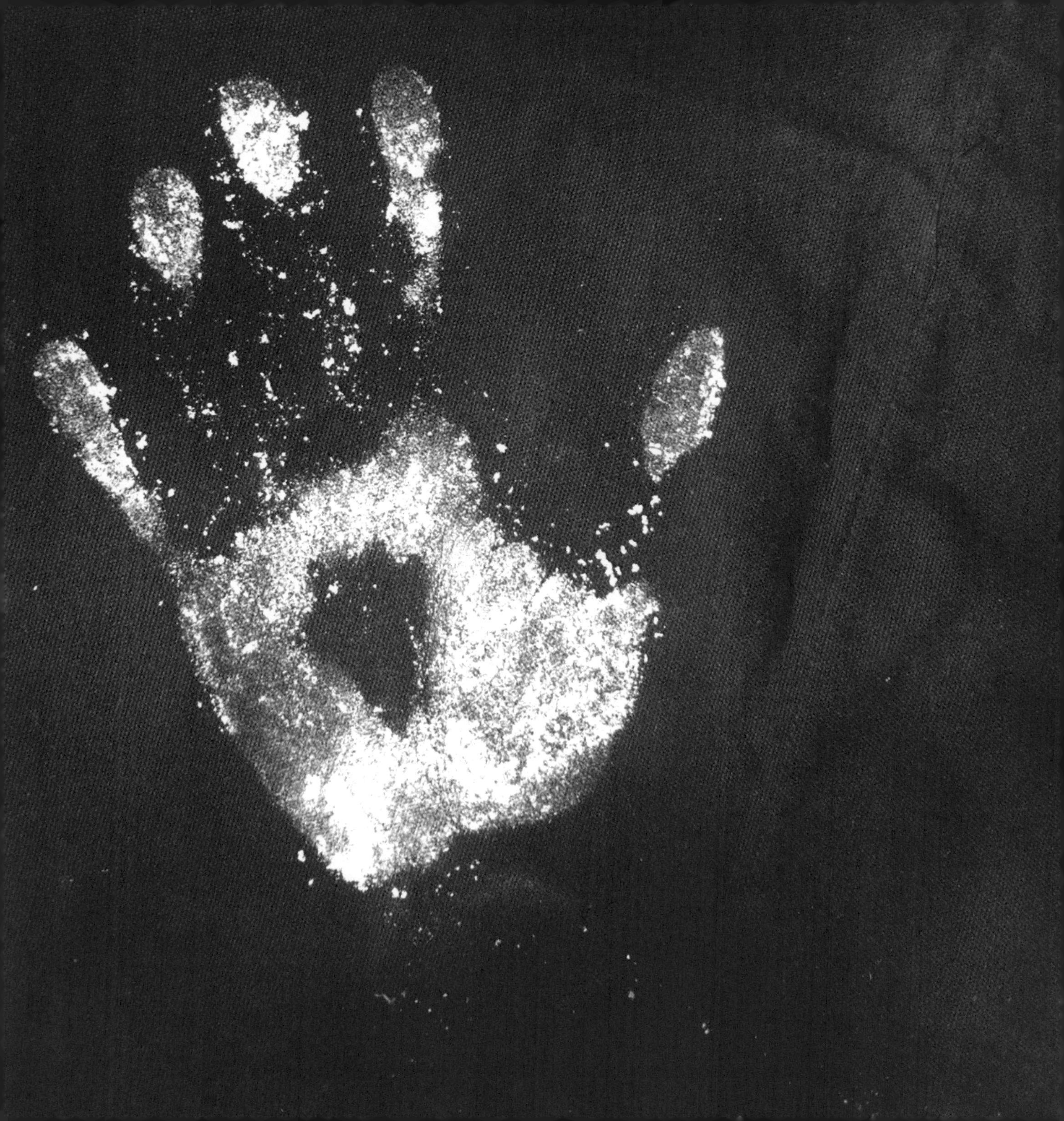

People

One of - if not the - most important assets a business or organisation has is its people. Those in charge of the most successful operations recognise that they rely upon having the right people with the right skills and right attitude. The best businesses will value and nurture their people, helping them to develop personally and professionally.

Look after your staff while showing who is in charge - don't leave them slogging with a wooden spoon in stiff dough if there is a mixer that will do the job better and faster. Provide them with a chilled water dispenser in the summer if it keeps them happy.

By all means be an artist or a scientist (or have them on your team) when it comes to baking, but keep a clear cool business head on your shoulders and set some clear operating rules. Don't let histrionic bakers or other staff members drive you to drink and ruin your business through chaos and disruptive behaviour.

Encourage your team to look smart and clean, but remember they need to feel comfortable in a hot (possibly cramped) environment involving heavy physical work.

Colin Hilder

Paid staff

A starting point when looking into taking on staff is to ensure that you fulfil your legal obligations. A source of information on matters including becoming an employer, recruiting and managing people, pay and pensions, equality and diversity, maternity and paternity, skills and training (including funding), payroll, health and safety and resolving problems at work, is the government site, Business Link: www.businesslink.gov.uk

Voluntary apprenticeships

This section is written for both the would-be professional baker and also the established baker that could take on an apprentice.

The Campaign believes that hands-on skill sharing is key to building the Real Bread baking community and the resurgence of Real Bread.

If you don't share your knowledge your craft dies with you.

Aidan Chapman

No matter how informative, books (even the lavishly-tooled *Knead to Know*), websites, and videos, there is no substitute for the hands-on learning experience of working alongside an accomplished professional Real Bread baker.

Some bakeries might prefer to offer a traditional apprenticeship, where the trainee is a paid junior member of staff over a much longer period, perhaps measured in years.

An alternative is the Real Bread Campaign's voluntary apprenticeship model. Going beyond taking on unpaid 'people to do stuff', the volunteer learns skills in return for their (increasingly skilled and useful) labour.

Length of the voluntary apprenticeship

A voluntary apprenticeship should last long enough to be of mutual benefit to the bakery and apprentice. What 'long enough' is depends upon those involved and what both parties feel is a fair exchange of skills for labour.

Emmanuel Hadjiandreou (whose CV includes a catalogue of well-respected bakeries in several countries, including Daylesford Organic, Flour Power City, baking for Gordon Ramsay, and most recently as head baker at Judges Bakery in Hastings), suggests that any less than two weeks of full-time shifts would mean the bakery would get little from an apprentice in return for the training it provides. He also recommends a trial shift for both parties to get a feel for whether or not the arrangement will work.

Clive Cobb at Town Mill Bakery in Lyme Regis feels that it would be a lot longer (two to three months or more) before the apprentice is able to begin to 'repay' the training he or she has received with semi-skilled labour.

At first, even though the apprentice is giving his/her time, arguably the greater investment comes from the baker. Not only is there value in the skills that he or she is imparting, but the baker also has to commit time (and we all know what time equals) to teaching and supervision, slowing production. The presence of an apprentice might reduce productivity even further by taking the workspace of an experienced baker.

Over time, however, the apprentice should reach a speed and proficiency in skills sufficient to begin to make a contribution to the bakery's profits, thereby repaying time invested in them.

Investment, commitment and respect

In order for a voluntary apprenticeship to work, the baker and volunteer must be prepared to make a full commit ment to it, agree and understand what each intends to get out of the arrangement and respect what the other is investing in it.

It would be unfair to a volunteer arriving with the understanding that he/she will be working under the supervision of a master baker, for them only ever to be given menial tasks alongside the least experienced member of staff. Conversely, it would be unfair to the bakery if the voluntary apprentice failed to show up on time or didn't follow instructions.

The voluntary apprentice must respect that the baker is passing on skills and knowledge that have taken many years to build up. Also, he/she must be willing to repay the time the bakery commits to training and supervision by maintaining a professional attitude, being attentive and doing the best job possible. The baker must respect that not only is the volunteer giving up his/her time and labour for nothing, he/she might be out of pocket on account of travel, food and accommodation.

Very importantly, the apprenticeship should be used as an opportunity for skills to pass on to a future professional Real Bread baker, not just unpaid labour or a free master class for a home baker.

What will be taught

This is something to be agreed between each bakery and volunteer. What each apprentice wants or needs to learn and what each baker or bakery is willing and able to teach will of course vary. Unsurprisingly, the Campaign asks that the bakery concentrates on practical Real Bread making skills.

Notwithstanding the notes above, an apprentice will be a junior member of the team and jobs could well include some floor sweeping or tea making.

Volunteers and the law

The following key points are adapted from Volunteers and the Law by Mark Restall.

Avoid giving volunteers income

Make sure that volunteers are receiving reimbursement for out-of-pocket expenses only, and collect receipts and transport tickets.

Reduce perks that could be seen as consideration

Any minor perks (and this includes training beyond that needed to carry out tasks agreed) that remain should be described as purely at the discretion of the organisation, rather than an enforceable right the volunteer gains as part of the relationship.

Reduce obligations on the part of the volunteer

It's fine to outline 'reasonable expectations', for example to express the hope that the volunteer can stay with you for X weeks/months. You can acknowledge that volunteers are free to leave at any time, but suggest that if they stay in the position for at least the specified time so they (and the organisation) will get the most out of the experience.

Don't make the relationship sound contractual

Avoid using language that smacks of employment. Terms such as 'contract', 'job' and 'payment' can be replaced by 'agreement', 'role' and 'reimbursement of expenses'. So, for example, rather than job descriptions for volunteers you might have role or task descriptions or outlines.

Make it clear that you don't intend to create a contract

For example, on written agreements, "This agreement is not intended to be a legally binding contract between us and may be cancelled at any time at the discretion of either party. Neither of us intends any employment relationship to be created either now or at any time in the future".

Create a distinction between paid workers and volunteers

This does not mean that you should treat volunteers as second-class citizens in the workplace, or that they should not be integrated into teams or departments. But it should be clear to an outside observer that the relationship between the volunteers and the organisation is different to that between the organisation and its paid staff.

Treat your volunteers fairly

It is worth noting that tribunal cases have occurred when volunteers have felt that they have been discriminated against or unfairly treated. It therefore follows that a key preventative measure should be to ensure that volunteers have no grounds to bring such cases.

You can find more information in Volunteers and the Law (ISBN 1 897708 30 0) by Mark Restall, published by Volunteering England, 2005 www.volunteering.org.uk

Confidentiality

The recipes and techniques used in a bakery are often key to its reputation and success. It's perfectly reasonable for a bakery to require that an apprentice does not pass on such business sensitive information to third parties, especially locally. It's also understandable if a baker chooses not to share the odd trade secret with an apprentice who will only be at the bakery for a relatively short time.

Talking turkey

Although the Campaign sees this as an opportunity to exchange skills for labour, at its discretion, a baker might agree to provide travel to/from the bakery, meals and perhaps accommodation, or instead reimburse the apprentice for such out-of pocket expenses. It would be up to the baker and apprentice to agree whether or not any given expenses will be covered, but if this does enter the discussion, please see the notes below on employment law.

Hopefully the agreement between a baker and apprentice can be based on trust but some might prefer to back this up with a deposit scheme. For example, three-month apprenticeships in which the apprentice pays a fully refundable deposit (e.g. £900 -£1000). After one month, the apprentice gets one third back, another third after two months and the final instalment upon completion of the full three months.

Employment law and volunteers

The following is intended to make you aware of the situation, not to scare you off. It's likely that the vast majority of volunteers would never consider claiming full employee rights.

Unless a bakery intends to take the apprentice on as a worker (who would therefore be entitled to full workers' rights, including minimum wage), the owner must be careful to understand the law applicable to volunteers. Two things to avoid are a contract (whether written or implied – you should work towards establishing an agreement instead) and consideration, which is the legal term for any form of benefit – monetary or otherwise – received in return for work.

Mutual understanding

To avoid misunderstandings and help the voluntary apprenticeship to be mutually beneficial (and enjoyable), we strongly recommend that the baker and volunteer apprentice meet up beforehand for a proper chat. We suggest that the following points are included in those discussed and agreed upon:

- What and how much experience the voluntary apprentice has.
- What the bakery intends to teach the voluntary apprentice.
- What the voluntary apprentice and the bakery hope to get out of the experience.
- The point of contact at the bakery who will be responsible for supervising the voluntary apprentice.
- Whether or not the bakery will provide services such as travel to/from the bakery, meals and accommodation, or will reimburse the voluntary apprentice for such out-of pocket expenses.
- What food hygiene, and health and safety training the voluntary apprentice has and what more is needed.
- Length of the voluntary apprenticeship.
- Times and dates of shifts.

It is also a good idea to exchange contact details (ideally mobile phone numbers) in case of any problems.

Example volunteer agreements

Should you wish to use a written agreement, you can find examples that could adapt for your own use at:

www.volunteering.org.uk/resources/goodpracticebank/Core+Themes/volunteerpolicies/index

www.standards.dfes.gov.uk/studysupport/816987/817959/filesandforms/form12

www.pavs.org.uk/publications/documents/VP1-SampleVolunteerArrangemnets.pdf

Peer-to-peer exchanges

Every baker does things slightly differently, so even if you are a baker already, there will be things that you can learn from fellow professionals or that they can learn from you. The Real Bread Campaign encourages members to host bakers from other bakeries and also to arrange reciprocal staff exchanges.

Suggestions for a volunteer agreement

Again this is taken from Volunteers and the Law by Mark Restall.

In an agreement an organisation might commit to:

- provide a full induction and any training necessary for the volunteer role;
- provide a named supervisor for the volunteer, with regular supervision meetings;
- treat volunteers in line with its equal opportunities policy;
- reimburse out-of-pocket expenses where there are receipts or similar evidence of cost to the volunteer.

It is also good practice to:

- provide insurance cover for the volunteers;
- implement good health and safety policies.

The agreement might expect volunteers to:

- follow the letter and spirit of the organisation's policies and procedures, including equal opportunities, sustainability, health and safety, and confidentiality.
- meet mutually agreed time commitments, or give notice if this is not possible.

Qualification and employment prospects

The apprentice should be aware that the sort of apprenticeship outlined here will not necessarily lead to employment at the host bakery, however bakeries will generally value this experience and demonstration of commitment when taking people on. The skills learnt during an apprenticeship at a Real Bread bakery would also make a valuable contribution towards the knowledge needed to set up a new bakery.

One of our long-term volunteers is treating it as an apprenticeship with the goal of starting her own bakery - she has volunteered for three months so far and we have arranged from the fourth month on that she will be paid expenses. Another chap is 58 and was made redundant and just wants something interesting to do. He got early retirement so doesn't really need any money. As well as their volunteer shifts they both now do a paid shift too, one as a pastry baker and one as our market stall holder on Thursdays.

We've also had 11 'one off' volunteers, which to be honest is really hard work and slows you down lots, even though I enjoy people's reactions to being thrown in at the deep end! We always get volunteers to do pretty much a bit of everything in the bakery and most people catch on really quickly.

We couldn't manage without our volunteers and we try to make them as much a part of the team as possible, including them in meetings, strategic planning and Christmas parties, amongst other things.

Dan McTiernan

Managing an entirely voluntary workforce

We have yet to come across one, but if your bakery is solely driven and managed by volunteers then it is good idea to encourage everyone to play an equal part in decision-making and running the group. You will need to recruit enough members to make the bakery work, and ensure that everyone contributes, so that all of the work does not fall on a few individuals. You may have a policy that all members are asked to volunteer a certain number of hours a month. It makes sense to designate specific responsibilities (such as managing the orders or the money) to members with the best experience and/or aptitude for those tasks. Another useful role is to have someone whose main task is volunteer co-ordination.

Matchmaking

The Real Bread Campaign is building a directory of bakeries willing to take on would-be or existing Real Bread bakers as voluntary apprentices.

Please get in touch with the Real Bread Campaign if:

- you would consider taking on a voluntary apprentice at your Real Bread bakery or
- you are interested in finding a bakery to take you on as a voluntary apprentice.

We'll then do what we can to put you in touch with a Real Bread bakery, or to put out the word that you can take on an apprentice.

The Bakehouse

A bakehouse is the place in which the baking takes place. It is interchangeable with the word bakery, though the latter often refers to the retail as well as production area.

What is a suitable space depends upon the type and volume of products you'll be baking and your business model. It could be anything from a domestic kitchen, a converted garage, an outhouse (e.g. on a farm or at a traditional mill), round the back of a shop or retail bakery, to a unit on an industrial estate. You might even share space - e.g. The Handmade Bakery rented the ovens of a local pizzeria, the bakers at Fifteen London work overnight in the restaurant kitchen between the chefs clearing down from dinner service and coming in again to set up for breakfast, and the E5 Bake House shares a space under a railway arch with two other food businesses.

We started thinking of public places that had ovens, like schools and dying pubs, and we suddenly realised there was an Italian restaurant with large stone-bottomed pizza oven in the village. We approached the owner, who was very supportive and enthusiastic and let us do some trials. Then we started the subscription scheme, baking twice a week during the day when the restaurant was unused.

We made sponges and production sourdoughs at home, carried all the rest of the ingredients to the restaurant and mixed the doughs there by hand.

Dan McTiernan

When setting up a professional bakehouse, your main equipment supplier may well offer the service of helping you with planning and design. This could perhaps include things like producing building floor plans and elevations, showing the proposed details on architects drawings, as well as detailed technical specifications for submission to local authorities requesting information on ventilation systems, or odour and noise control measures.

Considerations

When planning your bakehouse, here are some of the most important points to take into consideration:

- Production area (the place where you make and bake) needs to have sufficient space not only for the equipment you plan to install when starting, but also to allow for whatever level of expansion you may have in, at least, the short to mid-term. Don't go over the top and buy an aircraft hangar, but bear in mind it is easier (and less hassle) to expand a business, within a space than moving to a new one.
- Storage area for ingredients, preferably on the ground floor or with a lift if on the floor above. Should have easy access for receiving heavy deliveries, such as sacks of flour.
- Storage area for equipment when not in use. This is particularly important for a homebakery, as this should be kept separate from that for domestic use, not only to avoid cluttering your life but some environmental health officers will insist upon it.
- Somewhere for suppliers to park or stop temporarily to drop off deliveries.

- Separate equipment and hand washing facilities are required by law, as are staff toilets.
- Kitchen facilities (at least tea and coffee making) and ideally space for staff to take breaks and store their non-work clothing and other personal items.
- Arranging recycling, composting and other waste disposal facilities with the local council or private service provider. Councils can insist that a homebakery pays business rates for this service, rather than just chucking rubbish in with domestic waste collection.
- Electrical supply suitable for the equipment you're using, with an appropriate number of power points in suitable locations. Smaller bakeries may find that 240v single phase domestic supply is sufficient, but larger equipment may require a three-phase supply - your equipment supplier will be able to advise.
- Gas supply – you might choose this for heating, the oven or other cooking equipment – e.g. hotplate, grill or burner.
- Water, drainage and sewerage appropriate to the size of operation. Again, service providers may insist that a homebakery pays business rates.
- Ventilation – for the oven and production area in general. Planning permission may be required for an exhaust system, which will have to comply with building regulations. Your local council will be able to advise.

A single oven and some sort of work surface is all you need, although obviously the more space you have the more bread you can make. A mixer is not essential - I hand knead 50 loaves. In my experience oven space is the key limiting factor to my business.

Tom Baker

We're gonna need a bigger bakery

It is possible that your original bakehouse suits your needs for the final scale of operation you plan but many bakers will expand (either by extension or moving to new premises) at least once. Ideally any such upsizing will be anticipated in your original business plan.

You need a clean well-lit space. Whatever space you think you need to start with, at least double it as you'll generally very quickly find that space becomes an issue. Moving bakery can be a very expensive exercise. Think bigger than you'd think you'd initially need.

Troels Bendix

When we built our bakery we simply replicated the area that we had in our old bakery. In hindsight it should have been bigger, but we didn't know the way the business would develop in terms of the range of products we would make.

Peter Cook

See the notes in the *Trail of breadcrumbs from your kitchen* chapter for considerations around the decision to grow.

Equipment

The equipment you'll need depends on factors such as the type of products you'll be baking, how many loaves you intend to produce at a time and the space you have to work in.

We started The Handmade Bakery two loaves at a time from our Ikea oven at home. We bought some cane proving baskets, some plastic buckets of varying sizes, some scales and a sharp knife for slashing. We rapidly needed more oven space so looked for one already available locally and found our local Italian restaurant had a decent pizza oven, which did the trick for a dozen loaves at a time. For a couple of months we kneaded up to 115 loaves per bake by hand, but this got pretty tiring so we took the plunge and looked for a mixer. We found a 30 quart Hobart spiral mixer that had been cleared out of a school on eBay for £350. We got rid of the telly and plonked the mixer in our living room for a few months until we decided on getting our own premises. All in all we didn't spend more than about £600 on equipment to get us going.

We have now spent about £10,000 including a commercial oven and a bigger mixer. Space wise though we now bake in a tiny back room of a greengrocer's shop (3.5m x 4m) and currently produce 1100 loaves per week.

Dan McTiernan

Equipment for home/ microbakeries

Some of the following can also be useful in larger craft and artisan bakeries, though few are essential in either situation.

Baking stone

A commercially produced pizza stone or slab of refractory material. Opinion is divided on these: some insist they give a better crust to the heel (underside) of a loaf; others say that being only a centimetre or two thick, they cannot build up enough heat to make a difference. Also, referring to a loaf produced in a domestic oven but sold as 'stone baked' because it sat on one of these is not exactly in keeping with the Campaign's spirit.

Baking trays

The thicker the tray the better, as thin trays buckle in the high heat of the oven. Non-stick is fine but has a limited life when baking regularly, so you might find it better to used greased steel or aluminium.

Banneton

French for a proving basket. Usually made of wicker or bent cane. Sometimes lined with couche (see below).

Brotformen

The German version of a banneton. Can be made from wood pulp.

Cooling racks

Always cool your loaf on a rack otherwise the bottom will 'sweat' and go soggy. If you don't have a cooling rack, use something else that will allow air to circulate under the loaf, like the rack from a grill pan or the shelf from the oven.

Couche

Stiff cloth, often unbleached linen, used to hold softer doughs (e.g. baguettes and ciabatta) in shape whilst proving. Also used to line some proving baskets.

Dough scraper

Not essential, but a very useful utensil in bread-making: for many bakers, a scraper becomes an extension of the hand. Use the scraper to mix and cut the dough, lift it out of the bowl or off a work surface, and to scrape any scraps or dried bits off bowls, hands and work surfaces when cleaning up.

Dough trough

Plastic storage containers with sealable lids make good dough troughs for proving. They can also be used as mixing bowls. A 15 litre container will take 5kg of dough with space to rise.

Grignette

Small tool holding a very sharp blade (a lame) used to slash the tops of loaves. A very sharp knife can be used instead. The main purpose of a slash is to control where a loaf bursts during baking. It can also help differentiate similar-looking but different types of loaf, or one bakery from another.

Loaf tins

A deep-walled good quality metal tin will give excellent results and a traditionally shaped loaf. Always use a release agent to ensure loaves don't stick. Some bakers insist on using hard fat such as butter (though not if you want to keep it vegan) or vegetable shortening, while others say oil is fine. Pay particular attention to the corners and the neck (i.e. top part) of the tin.

If your loaf doesn't easily come out of the tin after baking, leave it for a few minutes and then try again. If it still sticks, then use the straight edge of a dough scraper to release the edges. This is normally where the sticking occurs. Don't be tempted to use a knife as you could puncture your loaf and scratch the non-stick coating of the tin.

Mixer

When deciding whether to invest in a mixer, you need to weigh up the cost of purchase, and running, maintenance and repair, against how much it will save you in staff time (i.e. wages) and how much it will increase your output and therefore potential income. On the latter, remember that the size of your oven and number of potential customers are limiting factors – there's no point in forking out for one that will churn out 40kg of dough if your oven only holds four loaves and you have only 20 regular customers in your bread club.

Mixing bowl

A three litre bowl is a good size for up to 1kg of dough. Alternatively, you can mix the dough on a work surface by making a well in the dry ingredients, pouring in the liquid and then incorporating the flour and any other ingredients from the outside edge.

Oven

Homebakeries generally make do with what they have, which might be gas, electric or even a wood-fired oven out in the back garden. The limitations of a domestic oven include capacity (i.e. how many loaves it will take), maximum temperature (you just won't get the deeply browned sole of a loaf baked in a professional oven), lack of steam retention (forget spraying water in or putting trays of ice or water in the bottom – the steam will escape, especially in a fan-assisted oven) meaning you won't get quite the crisp and glossy crust of a professionally baked artisan loaf. That said, most ovens (except perhaps older models) will still allow you to turn out a decent loaf.

We don't cover working with traditional (wood-fired cob, clay and earth) ovens in this edition of *Knead to Know*, but have included details of where to find information in the *Bookshelf, Equipment suppliers* and *Courses and training* chapters.

Oven thermometer

As the thermostats on domestic ovens tend to be inaccurate, a thermometer is useful to ensure your oven is at the temperature it says it is.

Scales

You will need to invest in accuarate and officially calibrated electronic scales to help ensure that your loaves consistently turn out as expected consistently and that they are the correct weight for sale.

Thermometer

For testing the temperature of the water and also the finished dough which, ideally, should be around 27-28°C.

I started with a second-hand commercial fan oven and a second-hand 20 quart mixer. With this you can produce small loves in batches of twelve or large loaves in batches of six. Also, six gastronorm trays or whatever fits the ovens, so that one batch can prove while the other is baking.

My own experience suggests that a 'small' (which is quite big by domestic standards) commercial convection oven and a 20-quart mixer with paddle, spiral hook and two bowls is about the minimum. I made a costly mistake over a mixer that wasn't up to the job before I got my Hobart.

Deck ovens are expensive to run and usually require a three-phase supply, which is itself costly to install and may not be available in your area anyway. As a bakery 'bigs up', three-phase probably becomes unavoidable. I have no personal experience, but I know one local food producer who bought a deck oven on eBay, only to sell it again when she discovered how much the three-phase was going to cost just to get it from one side of her industrial unit to the other.

Chose a brand for which a service engineer is available in your area, unless you are skilled in electrical and/or mechanical repairs yourself. I use Lincat ovens because the engineering is simple and spare parts can be had on overnight delivery. They answer the phone and they're British.

Steve Rickaby

Equipment for small craft bakeries

By Mike Hampson

Baking can be seen as an art, a craft or a science. Whichever your view, the method is as important as the recipe. The equipment that you use should ensure consistency by enabling control of the variables at each stage of the method and accurate measurement of the basic recipe. Although it is time consuming to formally record variations in your method, it will actually save time, wasted ingredients and lost customers. Starting with recipe formulation, ingredient weights must obviously be controlled, but so should temperature, which is often ignored. Time and temperature should then be monitored at the mixing, retarding and proving, and baking stages.

Selection of the basic equipment of the correct type, with a capacity to match production plans and reasonable growth that allows control is fundamental.

Scales

Once you upscale from micro-production, two or three will be needed. You must also use scales to measure water. A jug or bucket from the cold tap is not good enough as 5mm error in readin, caused by a tilt to the jug for example, will result in about 10% variation in weight between mixes.

Thermometer

Mixed dough temperature is largely controlled by water temperature and calculated by a simple formula using flour temperature (see the chapter on *Real Bread recipes and methods*), heat input from the mixer and the required finished temperature. As flour temperature and mains water temperature is likely to vary over the year the required water temperature will also change. The best solution is a water chiller and mixer. The alternative is the electronic scale, probe thermometer and buckets of iced water in the fridge.

Mixer

Vertical/planetary

From the Kenwood Chef and ubiquitous Hobart 20qt. to machines with capacities of 350 litres, vertical mixers can be used for heavy doughs to thin batters with a choice of mixing tools: usually beater hook and whisk. Although it is not the most efficient type of dough machine, the advantages are flexibility and second hand availability. Machines built before WW2 are still in use in UK bakeries.

Twin arm

Twin arm mixers, most famously the Artofex, have a slow action which requires a longer mixing time, double that of a spiral, and six or eight times that of a high speed mixer. This action made them unsuitable for the Chorleywood Bread Process, hence their disappearance. They are ideal for Real Bread, as there is much less heat generated than by higher speed mixing and the longer mix time can more easily be used to compensate for inaccuracies. They are now manufactured in Italy and can have two speeds and timers. Dough capacity is from 40Kg (which will mix a minimum of about 8kg) and costs about £7,000 new, compared to about £8,000 for a 60kg model. Reconditioned Artofex mixers are available, the smallest has a 120kg dough capacity and costs around £4,500 - £7,000.

Spiral

Developed in Germany, this is the dough mixer of craft bakeries throughout the world. Automatic two-speed timed operation ensures repeatability. Their relatively simple design reduces the manufacturing cost compared with a twin arm machine. To compare different makes, check that the bowl and tool are driven by separate motors, and then compare the power of the motors. Total machine weight is also some indication of overall durability. A 60Kg machine costs around £5,000.

A lighter weight version has been developed, initially for pizza restaurants, in sizes and at a price that brings them within reach of much smaller bakeries. Capacity is from 5kg to 44kg with prices from £1,000 to £2,000.

Fork

Primarily a French style of mixer, it is said that the forked tool folds the dough enclosing air, which lowers dough temperature. The bowl rotates due to friction between it and the kneaded dough. We have found that this is unreliable with reduced size mixes.

High speed

This type of machine, developed in the 1960s, uses high mechanical energy to develop doughs and is not appropriate for Real Bread.

Dough Development

Provers and retarder/provers are usually ignored or their importance under appreciated. Considering the proportion of the total process time of this stage why is it seldom considered necessary to control time or temperature and humidity? The answer is that you cannot do without a mixer and oven, but proving can take place anywhere. However, quality and consistency require control. This control is complex, therefore expensive and can only be cost effective in larger bakeries.

Wood cupboards with a gas ring and pan of water only disappeared from commercial bakeries because of fire inspections. Much of the equipment for small-scale dough conditioning now comes from France. The manufacturers have reached compromises between cost and sophistication, which are a major improvement. As a very rough guide, proving capacity should be two to three times the baking capacity. A 20 tray prover/retarder is about £5,500

Ovens

There are three methods of heating, all of which take place to some extent in all ovens:

- Convection is the natural rise of hot air. Often in an oven this will be assisted by a fan.
- Conduction is the transfer of heat through direct contact – e.g. from the hot floor of an oven to a loaf sitting on it.
- Radiation is the transfer of heat from one object to another by electromagnetic waves – think of a toaster, an electric grill or the walls of an oven.

The preferred mix of heating method depends on the product. For example a convection oven is good for pastry but a microwave oven isn't. Traditional ovens with a complex mix of all three heat sources appear to give the best results with bread products. Their thick walls are an excellent source of radiant heat, heavy sole plates provide a big hit of conducted heat to the base of the product and give strong natural convection currents. Unfortunately a stone-built oven that takes three days to heat from cold is impractical in most situations.

Deck ovens

The usual solution is a heavily-constructed deck oven. There are two basic styles of deck oven. Most common in the UK is the lighter version, which is not usually considered a bread oven in the rest of Europe. The ovens are electric and can be fitted with tile soles and steam generators. They are often of modular construction with each deck largely independent. This allows installation through a normal doorway and the addition of decks at a later date.

Output and budget will determine the choice of deck oven. The smallest deck oven will hold one standard UK baking sheet (30" x 18"). The price is approximately £2,500. A typical specification 12 tray capacity oven is about £15,000. The more heavily built ovens are also larger capacity, usually measured in a baking area of around 6m² or more. They can be electric or gas heated and cost from £20,000.

Ancillary items

Racks, tins, trays, ingredient bins, and a thousand smaller necessities will cost far more than expected. A figure of £5,000 should be budgeted for a small commercial bakery.

Apart from the oven and mixer, the only other important thing is tins, which are quite an expense - but we bought ours second hand and they're great. As to fancy gadgets, I find that a good sharp knife, a dough card for cutting and scraping the dough and a few simple bread baskets are enough, and a water spray for spraying baguettes - also handy for getting seeds to stick to loaves!

Feline Charpentier

Other equipment

Unless you are absolutely certain you need other pieces of equipment from day one, it is often better to wait to see proof that you do, rather than purchasing at the outset. Dividers, moulders, slicers, wrappers and so on can all be added to the bakery later, as required, to suit your products, output and budget.

Second hand equipment

In the past there were more small bakeries around and therefore more used equipment was in circulation. The machines were relatively simple and sturdily built with little use of electronics and therefore a long life expectancy. This started to change rapidly in the 1980s. There is now very little good recently used equipment for sale and there is a great deal that is long past its useful life. Age is not necessarily a principle consideration. Anything controlled by a circuit board must be viewed with caution and the availability and cost of replacements ascertained. Mechanical wear is much easier to assess and take account of in reaching a value. A sixty year old hand pie moulder is probably as good as and worth more than when new, whereas a two year old prover/retarder with a faulty control panel from an unknown manufacturer is worthless.

Reducing energy consumption

The Carbon Trust

If you are keen to reduce the negative environmental impact of your bakery, then cutting your energy consumption (and consequently your CO_2 emissions) is something you will need to tackle.

The Carbon Trust offers 0% interest loans to organisations to invest in energy saving projects. For details and to see if your business qualifies, visit: www.carbontrust.co.uk/cut-carbon-reduce-costs/products-services/loans/pages/loans.aspx

You can read a case study of how a Carbon Trust loan helped the Cavan Bakery at: http://tinyurl.com/62h2gba

Renewable energy suppliers/tariffs

Shop around to find a supplier that offers energy that will have a lower negative environmental impact. Examples include:

Good Energy – only offers power from 100% renewable sources – wind, small hydro, solar and sustainable biomass, and topped a September 2008 report by Ethical Consumer magazine.

www.goodenergy.co.uk
www.ethicalconsumer.org/FreeBuyersGuides/energyutilities/greenelectricitysuppliers.aspx

Ecotricity – in 2009, around 45% of Ecotricity's fuel mix was 'green' (including wind and biogas) and they continue to work towards 100% www.ecotricity.co.uk

Inspired by Pain Canevet in Brittany (www.paincanevet.com), we've just installed a 3.4 kW photovoltaic roof. It won't pay for itself until I'm dead, but the satisfaction of being able to put 'Baked with Sunshine' on our promotional material is worth it. 'Eco-bling', as someone recently and elegantly put it.

Steve Rickaby

A note on packaging

When choosing packaging, consider any negative impacts its production and disposal might have. What options do you have to reduce packaging that has involved the use of non-renewable materials, pollutants, high levels of energy and cannot be either reused or recycled?

This is a tricky area – e.g. a biodegradable cornstarch film might seem the perfect alternative to plastic, but how far has that corn come, what chemicals are involved in production, is the corn GM, what petrochemicals were used in its growth, what was the water footprint of the corn, and was its growth taking land away from food-production for people who needed it?

A recycled, unbleached paper bag that can then be recycled has many positives.

Second-hand equipment

Disadvantages

The downsides of choosing used equipment can include that it might not last as long, be more prone to breaking down, be less energy efficient than newer models, lack safety devices (e.g. interlocking guards and instant brakes), some of which may be required by law. Old equipment might even have developed dangerous faults that are not immediately apparent. You could find that the money you saved by buying second-hand quickly gets swallowed up and even overtaken by the cost of repairs and perhaps having to buy a replacement piece of kit. Worse still, using an old machine might lead to a serious accident or injury.

You should always ask for an up-to-date electrical safety certificate, some companies offer limited guarantees on reconditioned equipment and if you shop around, insurance cover might be available for it.

Advantages

Some bakeries have relied upon ex-display, reconditioned and other second hand equipment to be able to afford to start up. For example, Duncan Glendinning of The Thoughtful Bread Company told us that the hand washing basin was the only new fitting they bought for the original bakehouse. For some, the maxim 'they don't make them like they used to' holds true and the older equipment has been preferable to that being produced now.

Apart from our proving baskets and some scrapers, dough knives and tools, all of our equipment is second hand. We got most of our steel work benches from eBay and our oven, bread racks and big mixer from Belmont Bakery Machinery in Bolton, because they had been serviced and we needed that peace of mind rather than the unknown of eBay.

Unfortunately lots of high street bakers are going out of business, which means there is never a shortage of equipment for sale.

Dan McTiernan

Massive cost of new equipment would rule it out for many potential bakers. This applies to the major kit like ovens and mixers. In my view second-hand equipment is essential; I wouldn't have been able to afford to go commercial if I'd have had to buy new. I paid £370 for an ancient Hobart mixer; the same thing new would have been about £4,000. Thank goodness for eBay. The saving on the oven was less, and I had to do a lot of repairs to it in its first year, so in future I'd buy ovens new.

The Hobart rep for this area told me that the only thing wrong with old Hobarts is that 'they last too long'! He'd recently removed some pre-WWII mixers from west country schools that were working fine but no longer met health and safety standards.

Steve Rickaby

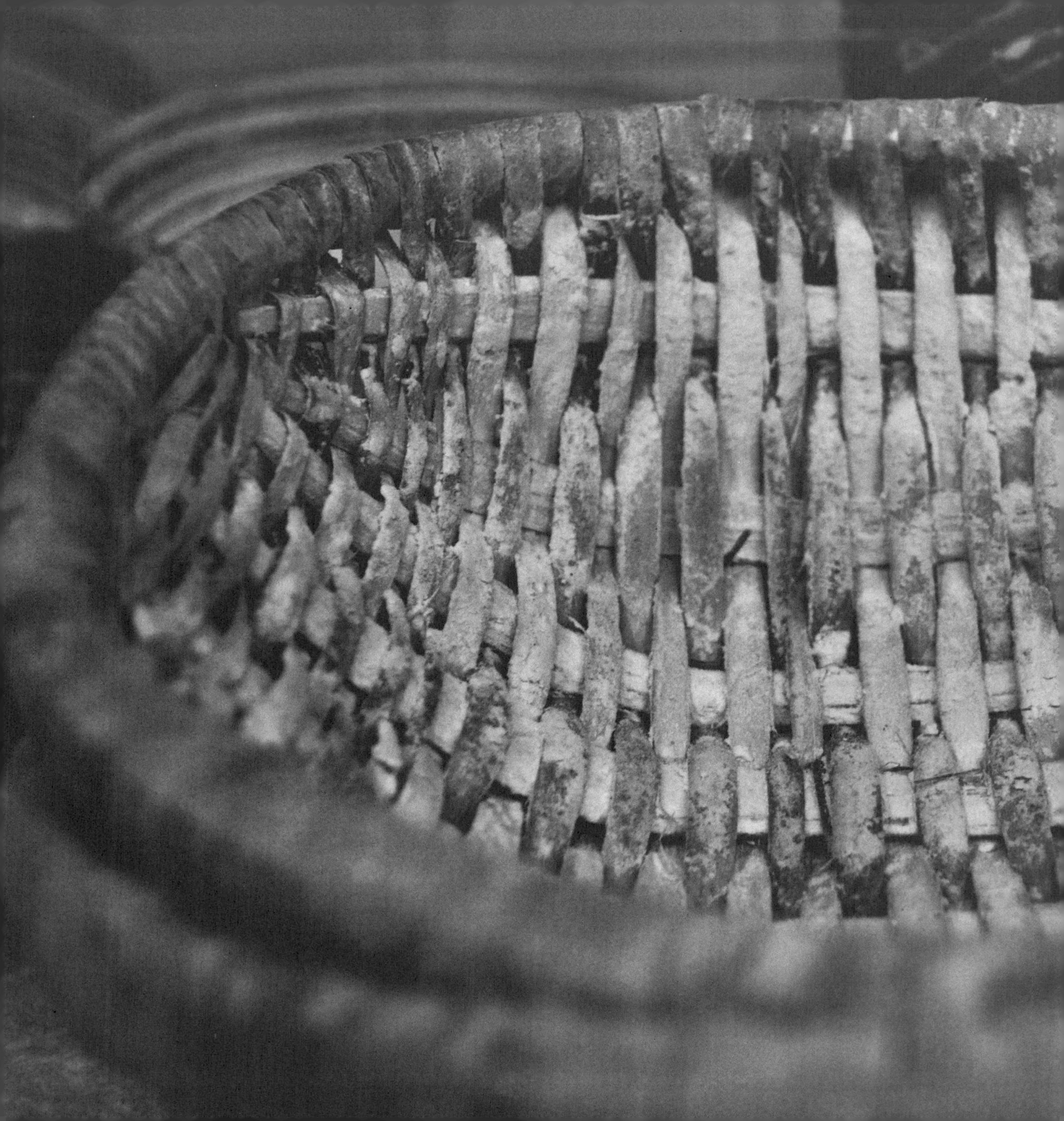

Insurance

The Association of British Insurers gives the following advice for businesses:

If you are in business you will need insurance; without it your livelihood is at risk. An unexpected loss could cause financial hardship and destroy years of hard work and by law, some types of insurance are compulsory.

There are three main areas where you need to consider the insurance requirements of your business. These are:

1) Insurances that protect against loss or damage caused to your business' property or trade by adverse events. Specific areas of insurance in this group may include cover for:

- Property – buildings and contents.
- Engineering failure.
- Theft.
- Money.
- Goods in transit.
- Business interruption.
- Trade Credit Insurance.
- Motor vehicles.
- Legal Expenses.

And a variety of other risks.

2) Insurances that cover your business's legal liabilities in the event of some aspect of your business causing damage or harm to a third party or their property. Employers' Liability insurance is compulsory by law, but other areas of liability that you may need to consider insurance cover for include:

- Public and product liability.
- Motor vehicle liability.

3) Insurances that protect both you or your employees against the consequences of serious illness, injury or death, and the effects these events could have on your employees, on their families, and on your business. Areas of insurance you might consider are:

- Personal accident and sickness insurance.
- Income protection insurance.
- Private medical insurance.
- Life insurance.
- Pensions.

You can download the full advice sheet, which contains much more detailed information on all of these areas, plus how to buy insurance and what to think about and ask for when buying insurance from: www.abi.org.uk/Information/Business/Insurance_Advice_for_Businesses.aspx

Product liability insurance can be costly: use a broker. Mine found a 'working from home' policy that threw in product liability for nothing though of course, I've not tested it yet!

Steve Rickaby

Insurance YES. And get cover for loss of income particularly if you are a one man band. If you have employees it is a legal requirement to have employer's liability and have ample cover. Almost all markets or larger shops will require public liability insurance for a minimum of £5 million. Dreadfully boring, but will keep you on the right side of the law. Also generally required by Farmers' Markets.

Troels Bendix

TWO
PENCE
ELIZABETH II

Money matters and admin

If you are just starting out as a small business, check with your local council to see if they run business information sessions. If so, these may include information on tax, banking and so on, and they may offer training sessions on bookkeeping and all matters financial.

You can also find a wealth of financial advice at www.businesslink.gov.uk

Pricing

Pricing is a balance between three factors:

- What you have to charge in order to at least break even after all of your costs are accounted for.
- What you want to charge e.g. because your aim is maximum profit or absolute minimum price to increase accessibility.
- What your customer base will tolerate – yours might be happy to pay to have a gift-boxed luxury loaf delivered, or consider anything much over 50p to be an example of 'rip off Britain'. Of course, the majority of people fall somewhere in between.

Here's an example from The Handmade Bakery of how to work out appropriate pricing:

'We have a costings spreadsheet which is split into ingredients costs plus all other overheads (including energy, labour, rent, transport and packaging). We then workout how much we can charge realistically as a RRP and work backwards from that to arrive at a wholesale price.'

Ingredients	Cost		Quantity		
White Loaf			**100**		
Flour	£25.50				
Yeast	£2.64				
Salt	£0.36				
Water	£0.10				
WAGE	£88.00				
Rates	£1.15				
Transport	£8.50				
Electricity	£3.50				
Rent	£10.00				
Packaging	£2.14				
Other	£12.40				
	£154.29	**Unit cost**	£1.54		
		Wholesale	£1.90	Cost %	£81.21
		RRP	£2.40	Profit %	£18.79
				Profit actual	£0.36

£160 (2 bakers) / 180 loaves per day = £88/100 loaves

It is vital though to be rigorous about costing your ingredients and time, so that you know whether you're running at a profit or a loss.

There needs to be a judicious balance between ingredient cost and market tolerance. I reckoned I'd got things about right when an equal number of people told me that my bread was too cheap as told me that it was too expensive! Be aware that third-party outlets will expect a wholesale price, which eats into your margins.

I'm fortunate (or unfortunate, depending on your point of view) to be computer-literate, so I have PC-based accounting running already. Everything else (recipes, batch size calculations, invoices and so on) is done using a giant spreadsheet, but I'm outgrowing this way of working.

Steve Rickaby

With handmade artisan bread the biggest production cost is always going to be labour and we try to pay our bakers a reasonable rate (£8.50 per hour currently). We also use organic ingredients, which are more expensive than non-organic but we believe the price is worth paying. Our 800g loaf range between £2.40 and £2.90 retail and we have never had anyone complain that they are over-priced, as far as we are aware.

Dan McTiernan

Remember that added ingredients such as fruit, seeds and nuts can be disproportionately expensive. Are your costings and selling prices truly reflecting this added cost and added value?

Understand your fixed and variable cost matrix (e.g. organic ingredients can cost two to four times as much as non-organic, but your equipment, labour, distribution and energy costs are the same) so use spreadsheets to keep track.

If you are in a niche market offering exceptional quality through specialist outlets then charge an appropriate price - don't try to enter into a price war with supermarkets.

Colin Hilder

Do not price yourselves too low at the beginning, as you are producing a quality product that shouldn't be undervalued.

John Letts

Taking payment

In order to maximise sales, you need to offer payment methods that best suit the majority of your customers. People buying a loaf or two from a homebakery, market stall and perhaps even a small retail bakery, in fact making purchases up to the value of £10, will generally prefer to pay in cash.

However, if you operate a subscription scheme, have an eat-in option, have a significant number of customers who buy in larger quantities, or offer added value and/or higher cost items (like cakes, sandwiches or coffee), you should consider taking cards and/or cheques. If you sell products wholesale, you may also need to set up direct payment (BACS, Direct Debit, standing orders etc.) and credit account facilities for your customers. Another possibility is online payments.

We are pretty unsophisticated. We take cash, cheque or payment by BACS. We have dabbled with PayPal but the margins on bread are so low that the fees are too high for us at the moment.

Because we are a workers' co-operative and a member of Co-operatives UK, we get free business banking with the Co-operative Bank.

Dan McTiernan

For a useful summary of the pros and cons of these different payment types and an outline of how to set up systems, such as a merchant credit/debit card account and online payment, see:

www.tourismnortheast.co.uk/site/business-toolkit/finance-and-funding/taking-payments

Your bank will also be able to provide advice but when setting up a business account, it is wise to shop around to compare their rates (fees and interest) and the type and level of support each will provide.

Cash handling procedures

- Always ensure you have a cash float, ideally of the same amount and preferably checked by two people at the start and end of the day/shift.
- Count up the money taken at the end of the day/shift and record this. This should then be double-checked.
- When counting cash, you need a secure space with a surface on which to count and bag up the money. Ideally, this will be away from the view of customers.
- Banks require coins bagged up with the types of coins and in the amounts specified on their plastic coin bags.
- Pay your takings into the bank as soon as possible, so that they appear both in your financial records and on your bank statement on the same date.
- If you need to keep any cash from one day to the next, make sure you have somewhere secure to store it, such as a lockable cash box or safe.
- If a supplier insists on payment in cash, ensure that you get a receipt.
- Ideally, no cash payments should ever be made other than through petty cash. Never make payments directly from cash received.

Taking payment as a wholesaler

Colin Hilder advises:

Collecting cash on delivery is good for cash flow but delays the driver, is prone to error or pilfering, is not easily auditable, takes ages to reconcile back at base, and costs a significant percentage to bank.

Putting customers on a credit account basis means that you can control the sales ledger and amount due but you must be tight on terms and insist on prompt payment – weekly or fortnightly is better than monthly. Also consider asking for (or offering) debit card facility, but remember it will cost you a premium of 1 to 3 % and could have relatively high costs for terminal hire and compliance, as well as long minimum contracts.

Card payments at farmers' markets

FARMA offers a co-operative card payment handling scheme for members. Terms are 1.1% for all consumer credit cards and debit card handling starts at 10p per transaction. Mobile machines for use in farmers' markets, catering sites and other outside venues are available.

'Alternative' forms of payment

Although it's unlikely that you could turn a bread barter into a successful and sustainable business model (but if you do, please let us know how so that we can share the knowledge), this could form at least part of your operation.

Ideas and examples:

- Ingredients – The Loaf in Crich gets a few pints of real ale from the local pub to use in barm and beer bread in exchange for a loaf or two each week; The Thoughtful Bread Company invites customers to bring in certain ingredients it needs for seasonal special loaves from their gardens, allotments, orchards or foraging trips in exchange for a discount.
- Labour – The Handmade Bakery is one of a number that have offered loaves in exchange for help at the bakery.
- Space and facilities – could you come to an arrangement to use bread to pay (or at least in part) for these?

See also the chapter on *Community Supported Baking*.

If you do wholesale, I strongly suggest you set out terms and conditions of sale and clearly state what credit terms you wish. It is wise from a cash flow perspective as a start-up to solely do cash on delivery and only later move onto credit terms. Be strict with the credit terms and do not be afraid to withhold supply if there is no payment. Accept all kinds of payment but make sure that when you open your bank account to get a long free banking period so you won't be charged for depositing cheques and cash. Encourage electronic payments.

Troels Bendix

VAT

If your turnover of VAT taxable goods and services supplied within the UK for the previous 12 months is more than the current registration threshold of £70,000, you must register for VAT. If taking over an existing business, you have to add your own VAT taxable turnover over the last 12 months (if any) to that of the business you're taking over. If the total goes over the registration threshold on the day of the takeover (currently £70,000), you'll have to register.

For the current details on VAT (including calculating your VAT taxable turnover, how to register, and the difference between goods/services that are zero rated and exempt) visit:

www.hmrc.gov.uk/vat/
www.businesslink.gov.uk/bdotg/action/layer?topicId=1073859188

Income tax and National Insurance

If you start working for yourself, you must register with HM Revenue & Customs as self-employed, even if you already send in a tax return. Even if you're not paying tax, if you fail to register within three months of self-employment, you could be liable to a fine.

If you need guidance concerning income tax and National Insurance, HM Revenue & Customs offers a range of courses to help. Their local workshops are designed specifically for people who are starting, or about to start, self-employment. These are free of charge and generally last no more than half a day. They also offer a one-to-one service to discuss any difficulties you may be having.

In addition, HM Revenue & Customs has a helpline specifically for new businesses: www.hmrc.gov.uk/businesses/tmastarting-up-in-business.shtml. See also: www.businesslink.gov.uk/bdotg/action/layer?&topicId=1074454203

Accounts and other admin

You need to have good administrative systems to keep records of orders you have placed with suppliers, orders you have taken, sales, and also contact details for customers.

There are a variety you could use including:

- Paper-based systems.
- Computer systems (e.g. Excel, QuickBooks, Microsoft Office invoice templates).
- Web-based databases.

Paper

Advantages: simple, cheap, doesn't need access to a computer or any technical knowledge.

Disadvantages: difficult to create a backup copy (other than carbon paper or making photocopies), time consuming, calculations have to be done manually, takes longer to send to another party (e.g. your accountant), and harder to update and make corrections.

Computer

Advantages: the data is in a standardised format, easy to e-mailed to others, easy to cut and paste information from other spreadsheets, e.g. previous accounts or catalogues from suppliers, can be used to perform a variety of calculations as well as storing information.

Disadvantages: you need to have a computer, buy a copy of the software, some IT skills, although spreadsheets are relatively easy to use.

We use QuickBooks and have an accountant to do our payroll and end of year accounts. We started, however, with a simple income/expenditure spreadsheet plus an invoice template from Microsoft Word. We could quite easily have stuck with that as QuickBooks takes a fair bit of learning!

Dan McTiernan

Web

Having a web-based database allows your customers to place their orders and pay online. Most web-based systems will manage all finances as well as customer details and orders and also have other functions such as enabling you to print off invoices. This sort of system is good if you have large numbers of customers and also if you have several different outlets or multiple drop-offs.

The main advantage is that all your orders will be handled by one system rather than lots of different spreadsheets and databases. Also, if designed well they are generally easy to use.

The main disadvantage is that anyone using the system needs to have Internet access. There is also always a cost whenever a payment is made on-line, as payment systems like PayPal charge a fee per order and a percentage of the cost. Therefore, a pay online facility is really only cost effective if you are taking a lot of orders. However, it is also possible for people to order online but still pay by cash, cheque or standing order. A web-based system may also cost quite a lot to develop and there will be an on-going web hosting cost.

Make sure you set up a computer-based accounts system, e.g. Microsoft Money and Intuit QuickBooks are free and can be quite adequate, or if you want to buy a package then TAS Books is an option. Unless you are convinced it is essential, consider very carefully before buying a more complex system such as Sage, even if the accountant pushes. You can look into baker specific software, which converts your recipes and customer orders into dough types and quantities for production and then monitors your ingredients call off and purchasing needs.

Colin Hilder

Sources of grants, loans and other funding for bakeries

Regional Development Agencies and Local Authorities

Although Regional Development Agencies (RDAs) are due to be abolished by March 2012, it might be worth asking yours if they can still offer any sort of grant or loan for which you might be eligible.

For more on the future of RDAs, visit:
www.englandsrdas.com/news/qas-on-the-future-of-rdas

Leader

One source of funding administered by RDAs (and also through Local Authorities) is the Leader (Liaison Entre Actions de Developement de l'Economie Rurale) programme, which is jointly funded by DEFRA and the European Union.

If your bakery is in a rural area, you might be able to take advantage of the programme as long as you can prove that your operation contributes to one or more of the programme's aims, which include:

- encouragement of rural tourism activities.
- the provision of basic services for the economy and rural population.

For example, The Oxford Bread Group received a Leader grant of £25,000 to buy agricultural and milling equipment.

For further details, including application process, visit:
www.defra.gov.uk/rural/rdpe/leader.htm
www.businesslink.gov.uk/rdpe

Local Enterprise Partnerships

When announcing the abolition of the RDAs, the Government also outlined the creation of Local Enterprise Partnerships (LEPs). These are due to carry out some, though not all of the functions of the RDAs. Additionally, the Government announced a £1bn Regional Growth Fund (RGF), which provides the opportunity for LEPs – and other organisations – to bid for funding. Designed to 'support private sector growth in areas where the private sector is currently weakest,' the RGF will accept bids from private/public partnerships that focus on projects and initiatives that will have an impact on jobs growth in the private sector.

At the time of writing much of the detail of has yet to be finalised.

For more on LEPs, visit:
www.bis.gov.uk/policies/regional-economic-development

Banks, building societies and other financial institutions

Shop around to see what sort of business loans are available on the market.

Banking

No matter how small your business, you will need to keep your personal finances separate from your business finances. Operating an independent business account allows you to do this. It is also of great benefit for your income tax records.

Adding an additional account under your name is straightforward with most high street banks. However, carefully look into the costs of banking. All banks should be able to provide an information pack on 'starting a new business'. Some include business planning and finance software. Most banks will show you how to keep a simple set of accounts.

A benefit of approaching the local branch of a bank is the value of their local knowledge. They will often know the locality, the people and often the market possibilities within your area. Plan ahead to have your accounts fully operational before you start trading.

Ethical baking

When you pay money into a bank, it will invest it in order to generate income for (amongst other things) the ability to pay interest and extend loans or other forms of credit. Certain banks aim for greater levels of transparency than others in declaring their investments and some have ethical policies in place to prevent them from investing in say the arms trade, fossil fuels or animal testing. Examples of banks with ethical policies include:

The Co-operative: www.co-operativebank.co.uk
Triodos: www.triodos.co.uk
Ecology building society: www.ecology.co.uk
Shared Interest: www.shared-interest.com

For information and independent ethical ratings of banks, visit:

www.ethicalconsumer.org
www.makewealthhistory.org/2009/01/06/which-is-the-most-ethical-bank/

Funding for Community Supported Bakeries

As not-for-profit or social enterprises (the latter being a profit-making business that also has generating a positive social outcome as a core purpose) you might be eligible for funding from sources other than a bank loan.

A grant could help you get the equipment you need to get started or cover additional costs to enable you to expand. However if you want your CSB to be sustainable in the long term it is important not to be reliant on external funding. Therefore, if you are getting funding for your core running costs it's important that you have plans for how to cover these once the funding has run out, for example through generating income from sales or perhaps running bread making courses.

Small grants up to £500 or £1000 – these can be very useful for getting funding for the basic equipment to run a homebakery. Small grants schemes are run by some local councils and there may also be a charitable trust in your area that will support local community projects.

Medium grants up to £20,000 – Normally these schemes have quite a quick turnaround and so you will hopefully hear if your bid has been successful within about eight weeks. The application forms and reporting procedures will generally be a bit longer than for small grants but should still not be too onerous. It may be easier to get funding for capital expenditure, e.g. for buying items of equipment, vans or other costly items, than it is to get funding for revenue, e.g. paying salaries or rent.

Large grants over £20,000 up to £300,000 or more - generally if you want to cover the costs of salaries and get funding for several years you will need to apply for a large grant. Usually funders will prefer to give large grants to projects that already have some history of managing funding and so it is a good idea to apply for smaller grants first and apply for more money as you develop and expand. Applying for large grants requires a lot of time and effort, and they can take up to six months to complete, especially if you have to write a bid alongside doing your day-to-day work. You will need to put in a very detailed budget, come up with milestones and outcomes and usually submit a business plan as well.

Here are a few of the many sources of information on funding that you might find useful:

Funding Central

Website from the National Council of Voluntary Organisations (NCVO) and The Office for the Third Sector (OTS). Offers comprehensive information about national, local and regional government funding, national, local or regional charitable funding, and EU funding.
www.fundingcentral.org.uk

Grassroots Grants

Offers small grants (£250 to a maximum total of £5000 over 3 years) to non-profit making, volunteer-led community groups, which have been running for 12 months or more, and which have an income of less than £30,000 a year. This is a three-year programme running from 2008 -2011 offering grants that can be used for general activities, projects or equipment. The funding is from the Office of the Third Sector and is managed nationally by the Community Development Foundation (CDF).
www.cdf.org.uk/web/guest/grassroots-grants

Local Action on Food

One of the benefits this Sustain project offers to its members is a regular round-up of funding opportunities. Discounted membership available to Real Bread Campaign members.
www.localactiononfood.org

UnLtd

A charity that supports social entrepreneurs - people with vision, drive, commitment and passion who want to change the world for the better. They offer awards - complete packages of funding and support - to help these individuals make their ideas a reality. The Handmade Bakery is an example of an UnLtd award-winner.
www.unltd.org.uk

See the *Bookshelf* chapter for links to further advice on and sources of funding.

I fought the law

...and the law won. At times, the process of doing things by the book might seem like a pain but make no mistake, doing so is not nearly as painful as getting caught trying to get away with not doing so.

Although there are hoops to jump through when you make the leap from baking for yourself to baking for others and again when taking on staff, most regulations are based on fairness and common sense. Because you are supplying food to the public, your business needs to comply with food legislation, mainly covering hygiene and trading standards. You may be inspected to make sure that any food or drink being sold is safe to eat and the description of the food does not mislead customers.

Before opening, get in touch with your local authority to plan your business, organise waste and recycling collection, get appropriate training, tools and advice – it could cost you more money if you don't.

NB: Please read the disclaimer at the end of Knead to Know. The information in this chapter was correct at the time of writing, but the relevant departments of your local council will be able to give you more detailed and up-to-date advice on everything in this chapter.

Registering your food business

Registration of premises used for a food business (including market stalls, delivery vehicles and other moveable structures) is required by the Food Premises (Registration) Regulations 1991.

Anyone starting a new food business of any size (so this includes homebakeries and CSBs) must register with the local authority at least 28 days before it starts trading. This applies if your business is operating for five or more days in any five consecutive weeks, so even if you only plan to bake once a week, if you do so every week then you will still need to register.

The process is simple: you just need to fill out a registration form and send it (some authorities offer online application) to your local authority. Registration cannot be refused and there is no charge. If you have more than one outlet for your loaves you may have to register them separately.

If you use premises in more than one local authority area (e.g. your bakehouse is in one town and you own/rent a shop 'across the border' in another authority's area), you must register with each authority separately. You will also need to inform the local authority of how many vehicles you use in relation to the business – e.g. for deliveries.

The premises for certain types of businesses need to be approved, rather than registered, including those using the following foods:

- Meat and meat products.
- Eggs.
- Milk and dairy products.
- Fish and fish products.

Food Premises (Registration) Regulations 1991
www.opsi.gov.uk/si/si1991/uksi_19912825_en_1.htm

Registering your business name

Sole traders and partnerships do not have to register a business name. For other legal forms of business, such as a limited company or limited partnership, registration is compulsory with Companies House. However, your product brand name and company name does not need to be the same.

Restrictions

To prevent unfair trading, there are certain names that cannot be used. You may not use certain words or expressions in your business name, such as Royal, International, Authority, Group, Prince and Princess, European, Fund and Charity, unless you have proper entitlement.

Displaying you business name

Your business name, the name of the sole trader or partners' names, and your business address should be printed on your stationery in accordance with the Companies Act 2006. This includes business letters, written orders for the supply of good and services and invoices. It is an offence not to disclose your business details as requested.

Visit the Companies House website for guidance
www.companieshouse.gov.uk/about/guidance.shtml

Food hygiene

Once you have registered as a food business, an environmental health officer (EHO) from the local council may visit your premises for a food hygiene inspection. Your premises include all of the rooms or buildings you use for the preparation and storage of food, including ingredients.

Don't feel intimidated by this – all home/microbakers to whom we spoke said that their EHO was very friendly and informative in helping them to ensure that they met the grade.

The man from the council came and conducted an inspection of my kitchen, which is where I will be baking. It was a useful, informative and enjoyable experience for me. I am more confident now that I have had the inspection and know what the inspector is looking for and how they can help me comply with legal requirements. Inspections are conducted every three months.

Devika Tamang

If you are using domestic spaces for your food business you will need to demonstrate that you are taking steps to ensure that this dual use will not compromise safety and hygiene – e.g. it is good practice to (and your EHO may insist that you) have separate food preparation equipment for the bakery and your own domestic use.

Things that the EHO will be looking out for include that:

- Your premises are clean and maintained in good condition.
- There is adequate lighting and ventilation.
- All food preparation equipment is clean, in good condition and easily kept hygienic – some EHOs may argue that wood is not an appropriate material for food preparation and that second-hand equipment is not hygienic but this is not universal.
- You have enough workspace to carry out tasks hygienically.
- You have appropriate facilities to protect your food from pests (and pets).
- Food is stored at appropriate temperatures – this particularly applies to meat and dairy products. The EHO may check that you have reduced the risk of cross-contamination in a fridge – e.g. sealable storage containers, raw meat stored below all other foods and no leaks or spills.

- Staff members (even if that's just you) have access to a toilet (or toilets, depending on the number of employees), which must not open directly into rooms where you handle food.
- A washbasin just for cleaning hands (i.e. not for washing equipment or any activity that involves food) has been installed in the food preparation area.
- Disinfectants and other cleaning chemicals are not stored in areas where food is handled.
- Any vehicle you use to transport foods is also kept clean and maintained in good condition.
- Items used to hold food (e.g. boxes and trays) in vehicles must not be used for transporting anything other than foods where this may cause contamination. If you do transport anything other than foods, you must keep the items separate so that there is no risk of food becoming contaminated.

Unless you are using meat or dairy products in your bakery, your local authority probably won't consider your business as a 'high risk' for food contamination or food poisoning. However, you still need to think carefully about food hygiene to keep the risks as low as possible. If you do plan to use meat or dairy (mmm - cheesy bacon bread…) then you will need to take extra steps, which may include food safety training. Your EHO will be able to advise.

Write (and stick to) regular cleaning routines for the ingredient storage area, production area, oven and other equipment, toilets and (if applicable) staff room. You should have routines for clean-as-you-go, end of shift and end of day, as well as even more thorough weekly and monthly cleans. If you don't, you will suffer not only from mould, mites, damp, insects, rodents and exotic aromas but also could be fined and/or have your business shut down or even face legal action from an unwell customer.

Food hygiene training

According to the Food Hygiene (England) Regulations 2006, the operator of a food business must ensure that food handlers are supervised, instructed and/or trained in food hygiene matters. A food handler is anyone involved in a food business who handles or prepares food whether open (unwrapped) or packaged. The supervision, instruction and/or training needed will depend on the particular job of the individual and the type of food that they handle.

It is not a legal requirement for all food handlers to have attended a training course on food hygiene (although you may want to offer this, especially if you employ more than a few staff), but it is important that anyone who is handling food to be aware of the essentials of food hygiene. If your EHO considers your business to be 'high risk', staff might need to receive more detailed training. Further training for managers might also be required.

An example of a form for staff to sign to confirm they understand basic hygiene practice and expectations is included in *Appendix 2: Basic food hygiene instruction form*.

As well as consulting your EHO, you can find guidance in a pack produced by the Food Standards Agency (FSA) called Safer Food, Better Business:

www.food.gov.uk/foodindustry/regulation/hygleg/hyglegresources/sfbb/sfbbcaterers/
www.food.gov.uk/foodindustry/regulation/hygleg/hygleginfo/foodhygknow/

Food Safety (General Food Hygiene) Regulations 1995
www.opsi.gov.uk/si/si1995/Uksi_19951763_en_1.htm

Food Hygiene (England) Regulations 2005
www.opsi.gov.uk/si/si2005/20052059.htm

Food Standards Agency guidance for food businesses on the Food Safety Act 1990
www.food.gov.uk/multimedia/pdfs/fsactguide.pdf

Planning permission

Unless using premises that are already in use as a bakery or similar, a new bakehouse will usually require planning permission for a change of use application. Anyone can make an application, but you will need specialist information (your equipment supplier may be able to advise) to help ensure that your application is successful. Retrospective applications and non-compliance will end up costing you unnecessary time, money and aggravation.

FSA checklist

The Food Standards Agency gives the following checklist of issues you need to consider when starting up a food business:

- Have you registered your premises?
- Do the design and construction of your premises meet legal requirements?
- Are you aware of the main General Food Law Requirements?
- Do you keep written records of all the suppliers that provide you with food or any food ingredients?
- Have you put food safety management procedures in place and are you keeping up-to-date records of these?
- Do you and your staff understand the principles of good food hygiene?
- Have you considered health and safety and fire safety arrangements?
- Have you registered as self-employed?
- Do you need to register for VAT?
- Are you keeping records of all your business income and expenses?
- Are you keeping records of your employees' pay and do you know how to pay their tax and National Insurance contributions?
- Do you describe food and drink accurately?
- Do you need to apply for any licences – e.g. for selling food on the street?

www.food.gov.uk/enforcement/enforceessential/startingup/

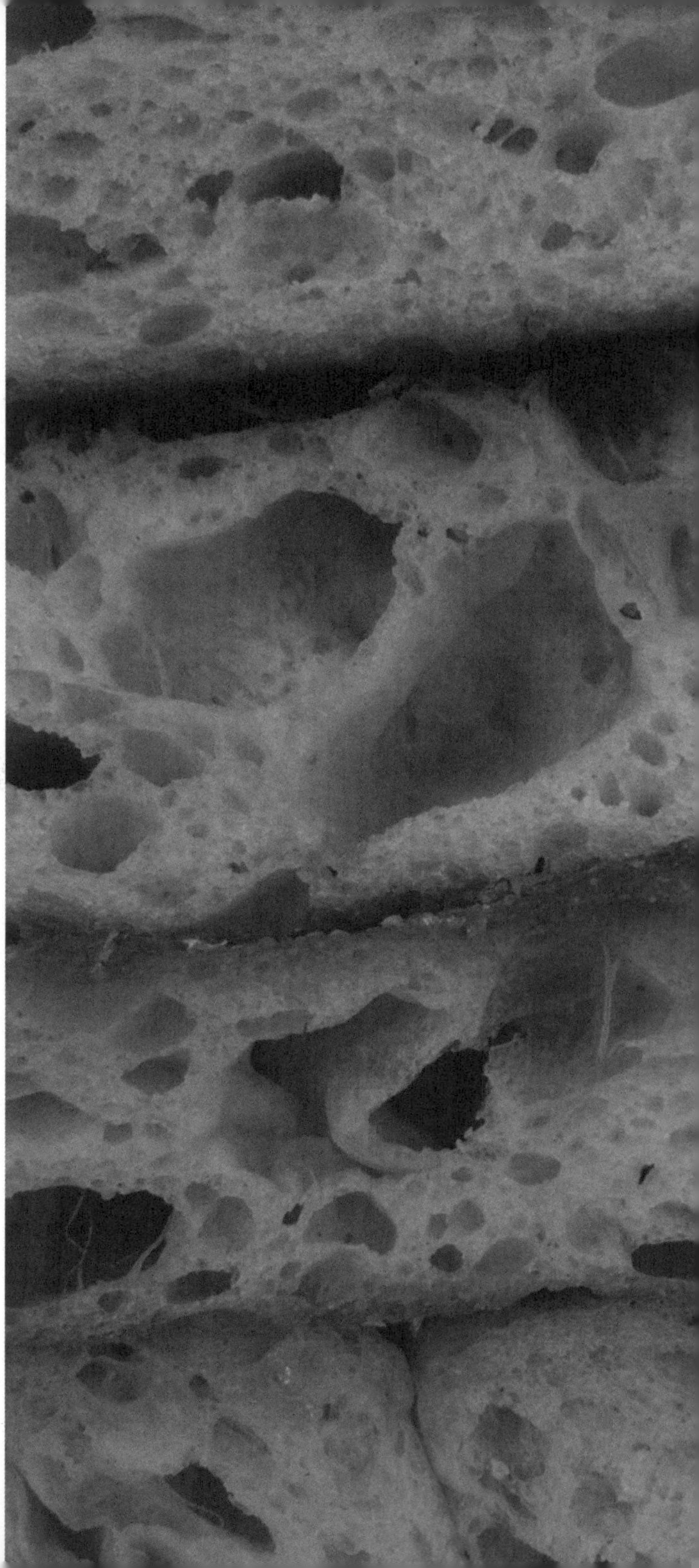

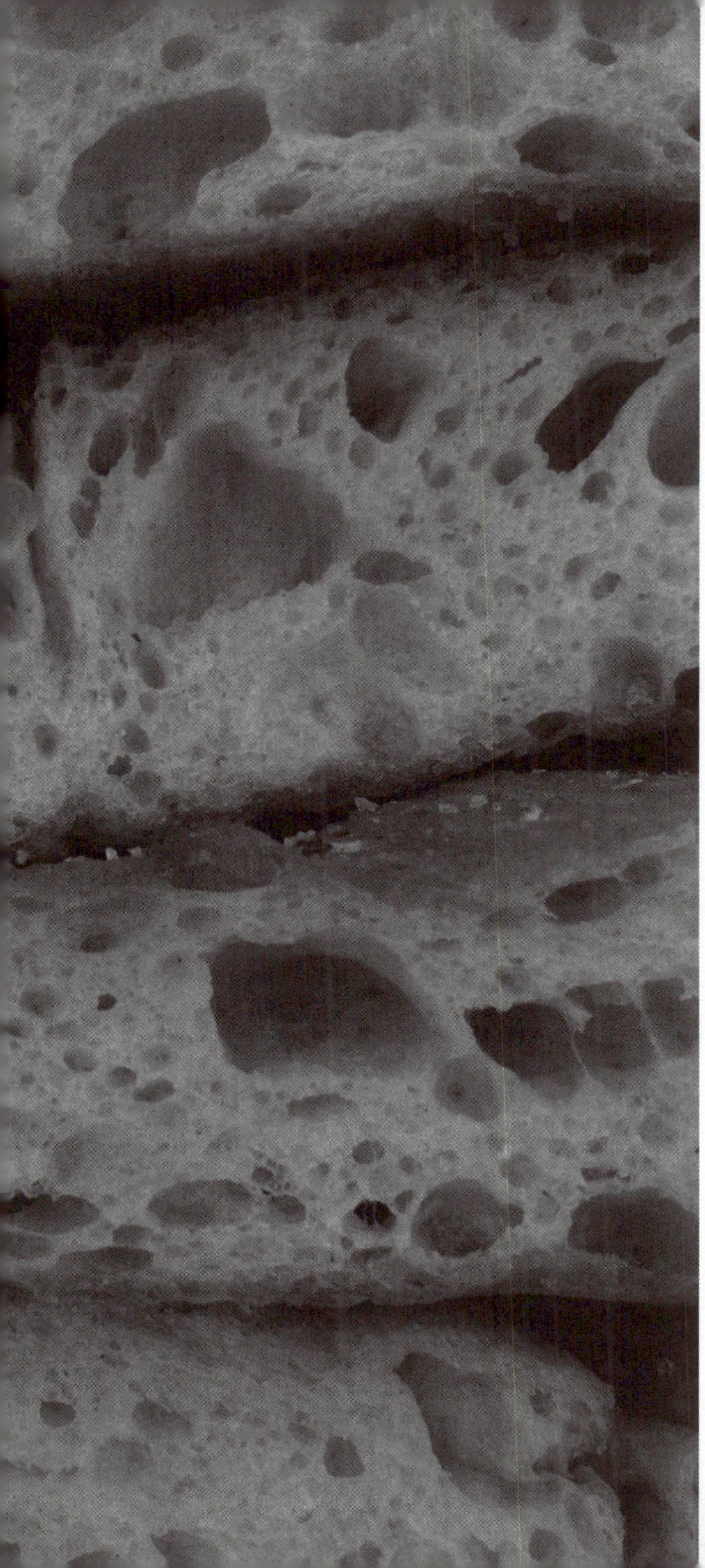

Street trading

If you are planning to have a stall or market outdoors then you may need to apply for a street trading licence. Street trading is defined as "the selling or offering for sale of any article in the street within designated areas". Anyone who wishes to sell items from a trailer or stall in a street must first obtain a Street Trading Consent from the Council which will cost a certain amount per year. If you are trading on private land (for example, on an area outside a community centre or church hall) then you may not need consent, but whoever owns the land may need Planning Permission. To confirm the situation it is best to contact your council's planning office. If you take a stall on a street market, the organiser will be able to advise you further.

Employment law and other relevant Legislation

There may also be other permits or licences for which you need to apply, and more regulations with which you need to comply. We have included links to some in the Bookshelf chapter and you can find much more advice on the following government sites:

www.businesslink.gov.uk/bdotg/action/detail?itemId=1083937186&type=RESOURCES

www.direct.gov.uk/en/Employment/index.htm

Trading standards

Weights and measures

All unwrapped loaves over 300g must weigh 400g, 800g or another multiple of 400g*. The same restriction on pre-packed loaves was abolished in April 2009 and you are now permitted to sell loaves of any weight in sealed packaging as long as this is shown clearly on the wrapper or label in grams.

All bread (packaged and unpackaged) that is sold in quantities weighing over 5 grams and less than 25 kilograms must now be packaged using the average system of quantity control. For example, for a 400g / 800g loaf this would mean:

- The average loaf must weigh at least 400g / 800g.
- At most one in 40 loaves can weigh less than 388g / 785g.
- No loaf can weigh less than 376g / 770g.

You must also allow for weight loss as loaves dry out. Loaves displayed for sale must meet their weight targets at all times.

See the section on Scaling in the *Notes on Real Bread recipes and methods* for a guide to dough weights.

For more details on average weights, contact your local authority's Trading Standards department for a copy of the *Small bakers and average weight guidelines*.

* At the time of writing, the government had just announced that it was reviewing the law regarding unwrapped loaves. The proposal is to bring the relevant Weights and Measures legislation in line with that for pre-packed loaves. If it gets passed, it is likely to permit unwrapped of any size to be sold, as long as a notice or label showing the weight (in grams) of any non-traditional size (i.e. loaves other than 400g, 800g or other multiple of 400g) is displayed. When and if this comes into force, the National Measurements Office is the department that will publish details.

Bread and Flour Regulations

The Bread and Flour Regulations lay down labelling and compositional standards for the breads and flours to which they apply. Much of this is more relevant to industrial manufacturers than to Real Bread bakers, though all bakers and millers should be aware of what the regulations say.

Bread and Flour Regulations 1998 (as amended):
www.opsi.gov.uk/si/si1998/19980141.htm
The Food Standards Agency guide to the Regulations:
www.food.gov.uk/multimedia/pdfs/breadflourguide.pdf

Honest (and legal) labelling

As we will outline in the *Marketing* chapter there are so many positive things that you can say about your locally-produced loaves to help them sell like hot cakes. However, the description and any other type of claim that you use for your Real Bread must be true and must not mislead your customers as to the true nature of the product. This is not only a request from the Real Bread Campaign (after all, we put a lot of effort into keeping an eye on the big boys falling short in these respects), it's also the law.

For example:

- You cannot use 'yeast free' or 'without yeast' in the description of sourdough loaves. The natural leaven in sourdough contains one or more types of yeast, maybe even including *Saccharomyces cerevisiae*, the same species (though perhaps a different strain) as commercial bakers' and brewers' yeast. An alternative could be 'made without commercial yeast'.
- The word organic can only be used to describe food that is produced and prepared in accordance with the detailed standards laid down and must be inspected and certified by an authorised body.
- Although the amounts and performance of gluten proteins (gliadin and glutenin) in rye, barley, oats, and the wheats listed in *a note on spelt* below are different to those found in modern wheat, gluten is still present, and so you cannot sell breads made with them as 'gluten-free'. An alternative could be 'made without wheat flour'.

- You can only use the terms 'wholemeal' or 'wholegrain' if all for the flour used is wholemeal, therefore saying 'contains wholemeal' on a loaf made with 25% white flour is not permitted.

Although there is growing scientific and anecdotal evidence to support the belief that loaves made using long-fermented sourdough might be suitable for some people with coeliac disease (an autoimmune disease, also known as sprue), or with an allergy or intolerance to wheat or gluten, this is not yet proven or recognised by the wider scientific community. The Real Bread Campaign is calling for more research into this, but for now, you cannot advertise any type of wheat bread as beneficial or even suitable for people with such conditions. If making such a claim, you must make clear that it is only a possibility e.g. 'this bread *might* be suitable for people who have difficulty digesting factory loaves' and then outline the current situation with research. You can find more information on the FAQs page of our website.

The guiding principle is that you should be honest and trustworthy and have evidence to back up your claims. If in any doubt, have a chat with your local trading standards officer.

Food Labelling Regulations 1996 (as amended):
www.opsi.gov.uk/si/si1996/Uksi_19961499_en_1.htm
Food labelling guidance on the FSA website:
www.food.gov.uk/foodindustry/guidancenotes/label regsguidance/

A note on spelt

Although with relatively different genetic structures to modern/common wheat (*Triticum aestivum*), spelt (*T. spelta* or *T. aestivum spelta*), einkorn (*T. monococcum*), emmer (*T. turgidum dicoccum* also called farro), khorasan (*T. turgidum diccocum* trademarked in the USA as Kamut) and durum (*T. turgidum durum*) are all types of wheat and therefore bread made with any of these cannot be sold as 'wheat free'. An alternative could be 'made without modern wheat'.

According to the Food Standard Agency's guidance notes for The Bread and Flour Regulations 1998 (as amended), spelt is: "...a cereal containing gluten and therefore a product containing spelt cannot be labelled as being gluten free. It may also be misleading to label a product containing "spelt" as wheat free as spelt is a type of wheat (*Triticum spelta*) and this would make spelt unsuitable for anyone with a wheat allergy or intolerance."

That said, some people report that they cannot eat modern wheat but find that they can eat spelt. Again, more research is needed. Some flours labelled as spelt may in fact be produced from a hybrid between true spelt and modern wheat, so check with the miller to be sure that the grain they use is pure-bred *Triticum spelta*.

Allergen notification

Food businesses selling food prepared or wrapped on site are not required by law to indicate whether it contains ingredients to which people may be allergic to such as wheat, gluten, nuts, milk or eggs. You may, however, choose to give this information as it will be important to some of your customers, or potential customers.

This FSA provides best practice advice on how to tackle allergy issues:

Food Allergy: What you need to know. A leaflet for caterers selling non pre-packaged foods:
www.food.gov.uk/multimedia/pdfs/publication/loosefoods leaflet1109.pdf
The provision of allergen information for non pre-packed foods guidance notes:
www.food.gov.uk/multimedia/pdfs/loosefoodsguidance.pdf
Food allergen labelling information:
www.food.gov.uk/safereating/allergyintol/label
Food allergen labelling legislation guidance:
www.food.gov.uk/multimedia/pdfs/publication/allergen labelguide09.pdf

Marketing

So, you're baking the best Real Bread that you can bake, right? Selling honest loaves at an honest price? You've gone to great lengths to ensure that each loaf looks, smells and – most importantly – tastes fantastic? Great, because the Real Bread's what it's all about.

Now, where are those customers? This is where marketing comes in.

What is marketing?

Marketing is more than just advertising. It's a process that starts (or at least should) in the very early stages of planning your Real Bread bakery or any changes to what you make and sell. Successful marketing can be summed up in Ps:

- The right **product**.
- For the right **person**.
- In the right **place**.
- At the right **price**.
- With the right **promotion**.

Marketing is "the homework that managers undertake to assess needs, measure their extent and intensity and determine whether a profitable opportunity exists. Marketing continues throughout the product's life, trying to find new customers by improving product appeal and performance, learning from product sales results and managing repeat performance."

Philip Kotler et al, Principles of Marketing, Pearson Education, 2002

We made a point of not paying for any advertising other than for printing of flyers. From our former lives we are fortunate to have design and communication skills in-house, so we do all our own graphics and photography. We made a big effort however to have a web presence from the start. At first this was just a free Wordspace blog that took just a few hours to set up. This was what we used for the first eight months or so until we got some Business Link funding to help pay for a web designer to build us a website. He used open source free software called DRUPAL.

Other marketing tools we use are Campaign Monitor, which is a neat and cheap way to create online newsletters which look nicely produced.

Apart from that we don't do much marketing other than through word of mouth. Our main key is to adhere to the Seth Godin (marketing guru) mantra of being a 'purple cow'. By this he means be remarkable. We try to keep pushing what we do and how we do it both to keep up our own ethical and political aims of trying to change our community's connection with food for the better, and because we recognise that only by thinking creatively and building on what we have done before will we be satisfied. By doing these things we have attracted the attention of regional and national press, radio and television.

Dan McTiernan

Two sides of the story

These elements in the mix need to be looked at from both the baker's and customer's point of view:

Baker	Customer
What loaves do you want to make?	What loaves do people want?
Who do you want as customers?	Who is interested in being your customer?
Where do you want to be based?	Where are your potential customers living?
How much do you need to charge to make your business sustainable?	How much are customers prepared to pay?
What messages do I need to communicate and how do I want to communicate them?	What story told in what way will make me want to buy from that bakery?

Marketing involves looking at the overlap between the answers to these two lists and finding ways of making that overlap bigger.

Marketing ingredients

Marketing can involve many different processes. The ones that we will look at here are:

- Market research.
- Promotion.
- Differentiation.
- Public relations.

And we'll look at media relations in the next chapter.

Market research

The 'market' is the collective term for your potential customers; the 'research' bit is finding out who and where they are and what they want. There are many ways of carrying out market research. Here are just some:

- Sampling – giving out tasters of breads you are considering making and asking which they prefer and would buy.
- A questionnaire.
- Food mapping – looking at where people can already buy loaves (Real Bread and otherwise) locally.

You can find more about food mapping at:
www.foodvision.gov.uk/pages/food-mapping

Questionnaires

Things you could ask in a questionnaire include:

- Where do you buy bread now?
- How many loaves a week do you buy?
- What types of loaf do you usually buy? (e.g. white sandwich loaf?)
- If you had the choice would you buy a different type? (e.g. wholemeal, sourdough)
- Would you be likely to shop at a local Real Bread bakery?
- What days and times would you go there?
- How much do you think is an honest price for a large/small loaf?
- Would you be prepared to pay a little more for a loaf if you knew it was baked locally without additives?

It can be more effective to carry out a questionnaire and sampling together, with questions such as:

- Would you buy loaf A?
- Would you buy loaf B?
- Would you buy loaf C?
- Do you think £2 is a fair price and would you be happy to pay it?
- If not, what do you think is a fair price?

As with any survey, there will probably be a bias in the responses as those who bother to fill it in are more likely to feel positively about the idea of a local Real Bread bakery. So be careful what conclusions you draw from analysing the answers. The length of the questionnaire is also crucial: make it too long and the response rate could be low. A short questionnaire of just a few simple questions could lead to a higher response rate.

We surveyed 150 people (Marsden and Slaithwaite Transition Towns (or MASTT) contacts) by email and found some useful information:

- *Our most important question was, "Would you buy bread from a local artisan bakery, and are you happy with the bread you currently buy". 66% said yes, and 21% said depending on cost and no one said they were happy with the bread they currently bought.*
- *Our second most important question was, "When would you like to shop for your bread?". 20% said they would like to buy before 11 am, but the remaining 80% were happy to buy bread after lunch until dinner time in the evening.*
- *We also tested the idea of the Community Supported Bakery and 62 % of those surveyed said they would be as, or more interested, in the bakery if it took the form of a subscription bakery as opposed to a traditional bakery shop. Most people were prepared to commit for a month at a time, but 14% of those surveyed said they would commit to 12 months at a time.*
- *Delicious taste was very important to people, supporting a local business also came up high, then health benefits, then organic and locally sourced ingredients.*

We also took part in MASTT events and a Christmas market. We were very happy with the survey results and the public feedback and based on them, we believed our community would embrace us and support us.

Dan McTiernan

The Food Co-ops Toolkit contains a whole chapter on market research. Entitled *Needs Assessment*, it looks at ways to: find out local statistics, conduct food mapping, run a community audit and consult the community.

You can download the toolkit for free from:
www.sustainweb.org/foodcoopstoolkit/

Promotion

'I shouldn't need to advertise – my Real Bread is the best for miles around!'

That may be so but thinking this way could prevent you from ever reaching beyond your existing customers. Even if your loaves do sell themselves instantly to anyone who tastes them, if there's a little extra expense or effort involved in buying loaves from you instead of somewhere else, even your existing customers might still need a gentle nudge from time to time.

So dust off that trumpet and pucker up; after all, the supermarket up the road isn't going to blow it for you.

Methods of and opportunities for advertising

- Chalkboard (inside and/or outside the shop).
- The shop window.
- Your staff.
- Shelf labels.
- Bread bags..
- Website/blog.
- Social networking (e.g. Facebook and Twitter).
- Information leaflets.
- Samples.
- Mailing list.

See the section below on *social networking*.

Differentiation

It pays to let potential (and existing) customers know the reasons for buying loaves from you instead of from someone else. In marketing speak these are your 'points of difference' or your 'USPs' – unique selling points.

So, what makes you so special? If any of any of the selling points in this chapter apply (or could be made to apply) to your bakery then SHOUT ABOUT THEM, but at the same time, please leave making false claims to rogue traders.

This is Real Bread

Baking Real Bread could well make you unique in your local community. The craft baking sector accounts for only around 3-5% of the loaves we buy in Britain. Even then, in a telephone conversation with the Real Bread Campaign project officer in 2009, the chair of the National Association of Master Bakers, which represents the interests of this sector, estimated that 80% of its members used artificial additives.

Point out to your customers that you are selling Real Bread and let them know that means:

- All natural ingredients.
- No artificial additives.
- No undeclared added enzymes.

Come clean

Although the law doesn't demand it, you should offer with your unwrapped loaves something that supermarket in-store bakeries don't – a full ingredients listing for every loaf at point of sale.

This even applies to any loaves that you also still bake using artificial 'improvers' (and that includes any listed on your flour), dough conditioners or other artificial additives. Your customers will respect your openness, honesty and giving them the opportunity to make fully informed choices. As well as helping to build trust and goodwill in your business, it could also lead to enough of them opting for Real Bread to give you the confidence in switching over all of your production.

Taste and texture

This is highly subjective. With at least a couple of generations having been brought up on factory loaves, for many Britons a toasted and buttered (or even marge'd) round of white sliced is comfort eating. The ad men told us that the shortcomings – pappy crumb, soft crust – were actually a good thing and as a nation we swallowed it.

On the other hand, many of us bemoan the erstwhile crisp crust, chewy crumb and depth of flavour of traditionally made Real Bread. Among the pap-o-philes, there are those who, through lack of availability or distrust of the unknown, simply haven't tried the real thing.

Cinnamon Square in Rickmansworth communicates how different production methods and times affect flavour in a simple and effective visual way using colourful Tasteometer signs in the bakery.

They also go into more detail in leaflets and on the website: www.cinnamonsquare.com/real_bread_takes_time.htm

Buy British

According to www.tora.co.uk/best-of-british-_1215.html:

If properly communicated to the customer, highlighting 100% British enables a brand to convey key benefits to the consumer including:

- Buying British: supporting British farmers will almost certainly capture the imagination and loyalty of the consumer.
- Local provenance: this often implies higher quality to the consumer as well as creating an emotional tie of a brand working within the community.
- The emotive connection of being able to visualise the farmer and environmental context that the food has been grown in (as utilised by supermarkets in their meat and dairy packs which show a photo of a farmer).

Bread Tasteometer

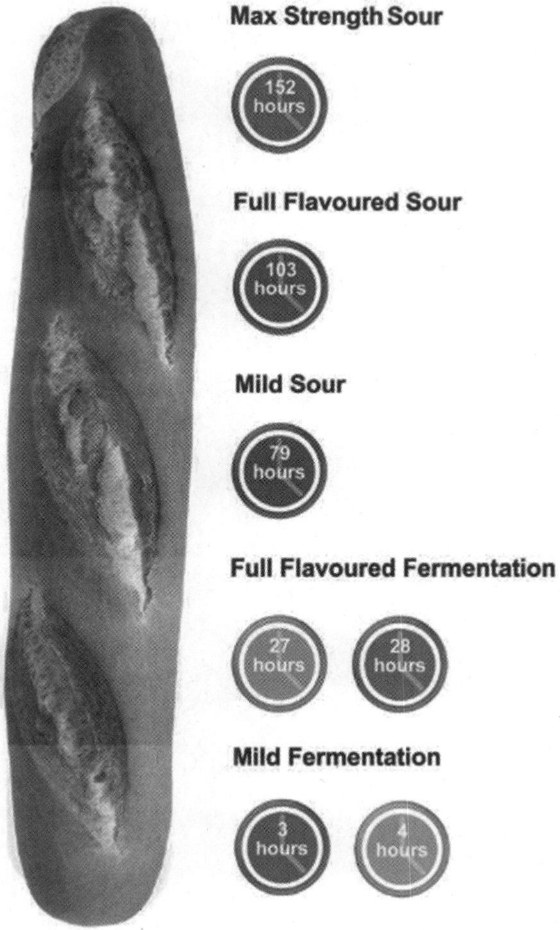

Better for your community

Is your bakery part of your local community, a business that offers meaningful, skilled jobs to people from your neighbourhood? Have you helped members of staff gain qualifications or win awards? Is the bakery a place where people, especially older members of the community and those who don't visit the pub (if you're lucky enough to have one) can meet and catch up? Would buying a 'value' loaf from an out of town supermarket make the same contribution to the local economy and community as buying Real Bread from your bakery?

What's the story?

One way of making a product more interesting and appealing to customers is by telling the story behind it. Here are things that might form the story of your bakery or a particular Real Bread that you bake:

- 100% British wheat.
- Locally grown wheat – if possible, say from exactly where and by whom.
- Flour milled locally - again, where's the mill and who's the miller?
- Flour stoneground by wind or water power.
- Other ingredients from farm X or dairy Y
- Wood-fired oven.
- Traditional local recipe – though please only say this if you can qualify it with information about its history.
- Sourdough – but if you are using natural leaven, please don't say 'no yeast' or 'yeast free' because that could bring your local trading standards officer knocking (see the *I fought the law* chapter). Go for something along the lines of 'no added bakers' yeast' instead.
- Longer fermentation.
- It's a family owned business.
- The bakery has operated on this site since / the ovens date back to X (though a week last Tuesday doesn't sound all that impressive).
- We bake for/once baked for X (insert major event, well known person or establishment).
- We're the only bakery in the area that still makes bread X in the traditional way.
- We've just revived the traditional X loaf.

Clare Marriage of Doves Farm has written an article to help you consider what stories you have to tell and messages you can send out to your customers to help sell your Real Bread - see *Appendix 3: Thinking about your Real Bread.*

Packaging

Colin Hilder says:

Well-designed quality packaging helps sell the product, informs and adds value in the consumer perception, but packaging needs higher up-front funding for minimum print runs and needs extra labour, care and cost of production.

Don't make the label too fussy. As well making the bakery's logo prominent, make the product name bold and self-explanatory, the weight bold and clear, and the ingredients listed correctly and in full.

Get to know your local packaging supplier and be very aware of cost. When I started I was using 'display' bags that cost 4p each. They looked great, but the cost was silly.

Steve Rickaby

Logo

Think of any successful business or product and chances are one of the first things to spring to mind is its logo. Make yours bold and make it clear so that it will jump out from wherever it's used, be that the sign above your shop, a newspaper article, a website, or as a tiny weeny icon on your price labels or social networking account. It also makes sense to have one that works equally well in black and white as in full colour – wishy washy grey rarely impresses. If you have a snappy URL for your website, you might want to consider including that, too. Lastly, try to 'future proof' your logo (and name, for that matter). A logo saying 'Millennium Bakery' in the latest font available at the turn of the century can only have looked at its best back in the year 2000.

Promotions

Ring the changes

Variety is the spice of life and alongside 'free', the word 'new' is one of the most attention grabbing in advertising. Are you able to bake a special, either on occasion (such as hot cross buns in the week before Easter or challah for Sabbath) or monthly or weekly?

Rewarding loyalty

One way of encouraging and saying thanks for regular custom is the occasional freebie. Here are some ways that might work for you:

Loyalty card – business card sized with spaces for you to stamp each time the customer makes an applicable purchase (which could be a minimum spend or a particular product) within a set time. Once the card is full, the customer gets a free product. e.g. baker's dozen - buy 12 small tin loaves get one free.

Sneaky bun – for particularly good customers, perhaps throw in a small piece (maybe a bun or a pastry) every now and then.

Food co-op discount – In return for them placing a regular bulk order for a single pick up/delivery, offer a discount to a local food buying co-op. See the reaching out section below for more on food-coops.

Advance payment discount – as used by some Community Supported Bakeries. Customers paying for a regular order in advance get a discount on the regular shelf price. This may be proportional to the size of order or length of commitment – e.g. an order of 5 loaves a week, would attract a greater discount than one loaf, or payment for six months in advance, would have a greater discount than month by month payments.

Reaching out

...also known as public relations.

Whether it's a stand-alone event or part of something wider, a Real Bread activity is a great way to bring people together. After all, we derive the word companion from *cum panis*, a Latin phrase that can be translated as 'one with whom we share bread'.

As well as making you feel all warm and fuzzy, events and activities that establish and build upon links with your local community are all part of the marketing mix that will help promote your business.

Here are some ideas:

Food co-ops

Join, set up or supply a local food co-op. A food buying co-operative is a group of people purchasing food collectively and distributing it amongst its members on a not-for-profit basis. It is a good way of getting affordable real food to people who might otherwise have difficulty accessing it. The Campaign can help you to see if one exists locally, or perhaps you could work with members of your community to start one.

You can find more about food co-ops at www.foodcoops.org

Bread competitions

What local event is complete without some sort of baking competition? From village fête, to harvest festival, to food fair, inviting people to roll up their sleeves and make a loaf is a great way to get people joining in a friendly competition with tasty results. Whether you have public or closed judging is up to you, though watching people nibble on twenty different loaves for an hour is perhaps a spectator sport for die-hard bread fans only!

- A flour show - Real Bread making competition for home bakers.
- Festival loaf competition between professional Real Bread bakers at an event.

We have more notes on competitions in the bakers' support section of our website.

Bread courses

These can not only help your bakery to establish links with the local community and be a valuable source of income, but also help share the joys of Real Bread. Anecdotally, several bakers have told us that the more that people know and understand about bread, the more likely they are to be loyal customers.

Lessons in Loaf

The Campaign runs this scheme to pass on Real Bread making skills in schools. Some participating bakers have reported that the hands-on experience has converted children to the delights of Real Bread, dispatching their parents to the bakery for more.

Bread making at events

Baking in a portable oven is a useful marketing opportunity, helping you to reach out beyond your usual customer base to potential new customers. Pizza might be the best option as:

- Kids (and others) can get to roll out and top the dough. You could even work in a from-scratch Real Bread making lesson.
- They are quick to bake.
- Even if sold at a very affordable price, they have a good profit margin.

Feasts and tastings

- Trencher feast – bake trenchers (medieval-style bread plates), then enjoy a shared meal off them.
- Breads of the world – if your local community has a mixed national/cultural heritage, hold an event to taste (and even learn to make) the breads from those cultures. While you're at it, you might also want to throw in some of the other food, music and dance to make it a feast or full-on festival.

- A local Real Bread tour – if you're lucky enough to have a wheat grower, traditional mill and Real Bread baker locally, you could even follow the whole journey from seed to sandwich.
- A talk from a local Real Bread baker, perhaps including a tasting of different breads and/or a demo of bread making skills.
- What other small independent producers do you have nearby? Team up for a talk and feast of Real Bread and real ale, cheese, sausages, or whatever is the finest local produce.

Other promotional activities

- To mark a particular local event, bake a special local loaf, ideally with flour that has been milled locally.
- Team up with other local producers to organise a Real Bread picnic for your community.
- Run a bread making class for a local community group – WI, youth centre, Scouts/Guides, for the regulars of the pub, or perhaps a religious group.
- Invite members of the community to visit the bakery in action.
- At Christmas, do a delivery to older and less mobile local residents.
- Work with another local producer/retailer/eatery to run a tasting evening, pairing your various Real Breads with other foods and drinks.
- Revive a local traditional loaf recipe to bake.
- A harvest festival with Real Bread as the star of the show.
- Bake a Local Loaf for Lammas at the end of July/ beginning of August (see the Campaign website for more information).

Marketing a CSB

As part of The Soil Association's support for Community Supported Agriculture (CSA) groups, Rob Greenland from The Social Business (www.thesocialbusiness.co.uk) ran workshops on marketing for CSAs. Much of this information is of relevance to Community Supported Bakeries. Click here for notes from his presentation: www.slideshare.net/robg/a-doable-marketing-plan-for-your-csa

What's in a name?

A good business name can:

- Reflect the type of image you wish to create.
- Clarify the types of products, production methods or company values.
- Be used as a brand marketing tool.

Simple, easy to pronounce, yet catchy names are the best. Avoid names that are difficult to spell, as this can create problems when a customer or supplier is sending payment by cheque or trying to locate a website.

If you are planning to have your own website, it is worthwhile trying to choose a name that is available as a domain name. It can be difficult to find a new name on the Internet, but you can use a domain checker to make sure that your idea has not been used before. A new name within your market will help you to market your business and stand out from competitors.

Similar considerations apply to naming new products.

Websites

Where do people go when they want to find a local supplier of something? For many years, flicking through a copy of the Yellow Pages or local phone book was the easiest option to discover local business services. Today, for many people an Internet search engine like Google is the only place to start.

An Internet presence is essential for almost any business looking to communicate with potential customers. A website can be a low cost form of advertising, which can be tailored to suit the needs of your bakery – from a very basic one page 'who, what, where' listing to a comprehensive online store.

Unlike paper-based advertising you can update your online information as often as you like for little or no cost. You can provide a rich experience for visitors by including news, pictures and even videos, giving them a reason to linger on the site and return in future. It also provides and alternative channel of communication between you, customers and fellow bakers when they are not in the shop.

Here are just some examples of the different ways that a variety of Real Bread bakeries use their websites:

www.hobbshousebakery.co.uk
www.loafonline.co.uk
www.thehandmadebakery.coop
www.nealsyardbakery.co.uk
www.pullinsbakers.co.uk
www.celticbakery.co.uk
www.phoenixbakery.co.uk

For more, visit the Real Bread Finder on our website and click through from a bakery to its website.

The best place to find advice about the Internet and websites is… you've guessed it: on the Internet itself. Various business advice services, such as Business Link, provide helpful guides to managing online marketing.

Considerations when setting up a website

There are many things to consider when entering the online world. Your budget and time are two of the biggest factors. If you have no budget for a website but have good IT know-how (or you know someone who does) you can create an impressive website in minutes for next to nothing. However, if you are new to website design, you may want to consult a web designing service.

Other important considerations include:

- Domain name – the address of your website. Ideally this should be short, memorable and obviously related to your business. You will have to pay to register this, which you can do through an Internet service provider.
- Content - Do you want your website to have a simple listing with basic information about your business and contact details or do you want something more sophisticated?
- Internet service provider (ISP) – how much do they charge and what support and other services do you get in return?
- Design – what will the pages look like? For example, pictures can brighten up your site but too many might leave it looking cluttered. How will visitors navigate around the site? It needs to be user friendly – for example, it's no good hiding your address away somewhere that it would take the user five clicks to find.
- Testing – make sure your website content is correct and up-to-date. Make sure you pages are easy to navigate and all of your links go to the correct place. Get your friends or family to try the website and ask for their feedback.
- Maintenance - Think about how often you will be willing (and able) to update your website content and design that content accordingly. It's no use putting a weekly special on the site if you're not able to update it on a weekly basis, or details of a one-off bread making class that's still there three months later. Do you want to add your latest news and product information to give customers a reason to return to the site regularly?
- Monitoring – there are many tools available which can tell you how visitors are using your site, which pages they click on and how long they stay. This can be very useful information to get an idea about what people like about your business and what you could improve.
- Search engine optimisation (SEO) – it is useful to ensure that the wording used on your site (on-screen and the hidden tags) match the keywords and phrases people are likely to use when searching for Real Bread. These might include, for instance, 'local bakery', 'bread' or 'sourdough'. SEO also includes raising your

search engine ranking – i.e. how high up the list you come when someone performs a relevant search. Some of the search engines themselves provide information on SEO, as might your ISP or web designer.

- Online advertising - You may consider using search engine advertising tools (For example, Google Adwords www.google.co.uk/intl/en/ads/) to boost the number of visitors to your site. One downside is that you can end up with unwanted advertisers on your site.

Blogs

An alternative to a website is a blog, which is a popular way of getting a web presence in a matter of minutes. Blogs are usually free to set up, have ready-to-use design templates and so can be mastered by anyone who is comfortable with word processing. Whether you set a blog up with information and images that you change relatively infrequently, use as an online diary/news page, or a combination of the two, is up to you. You can even include a message board to allow on-screen interaction with customers.

Both Loaf social enterprise and The Handmade Bakery used a blog to promote themselves before moving on to professionally designed websites once they were established.

Popular blogging services include:

www.blogger.com/start
www.wordpress.org
www.typepad.com

e-newsletter

A very cheap way to keep your business in the minds of your customers is a regular (perhaps weekly, monthly or quarterly) email newsletter. Contents might include details of new products, special offers, events, staff changes, and other news from the bakery. Build up a contact list by having a sign-up sheet on display at the bakery/shop/stall, or through your website, or (if in a business district) by collecting business cards in a goldfish bowl. A monthly prize draw can help as a sign-up incentive.

Social media

Many businesses, large and small, find social media useful both in establishing and maintaining real-life relationships, whether they are with customers, suppliers or people in the longer-established media, such as TV, newspapers, radio.

Starting a business can be a stressful and isolating experience. By using social media sites, bakers can meet others who are on a similar baking journey. You can find advice and support to encourage you and find new opportunities to market your bread.

Twitter and Facebook can give you an immediate response from customers. Many food writers and journalists use Twitter so it can be an excellent way of making contacts and getting your brand across to influential people.

Peter Cook

Twitter is essential! Well, perhaps that's an overstatement but it's been an invaluable part of my marketing. Through it, I'm now known locally as 'the bread man' and have taken lots of course bookings through Twitter. Lots of journalists are on Twitter, so it can lead to more mainstream opportunities, too. I can't believe that I can effectively text a question to Dan Lepard and he'll text the answer back!

Tom Baker

Social media use web-based technology to transform broadcast media approaches into a social dialogue or interaction. An important feature is the democratic nature of the creation and exchange of content – anyone with Internet access can get involved. The information you make available through such media can be text, images, audio or video. With many services, you have the choice of allowing anyone to read what you post or limiting access to a particular group of contacts.

The Real Bread Campaign, many of our members, and individuals and businesses in our wider network of supporters are regular users of social media sites.

What do I put on these social media sites?

As well as creating a profile on social networks, it is important to contribute by creating and updating your content so that people want to return to visit your profile again. This could be in the form of recipes, pictures, events, interesting news or even video clips. You should also remember that social media is not all 'me, me, me', it's about interaction in order to strengthen and enlarge your online relationships. Don't just broadcast your own information – if you see something interesting that someone else has posted, forward it on and someone might do the same for you, and take the opportunity to ask and answer questions. The Marketing Pilgrim guide to social media marketing suggests that while community is queen in social media, quality content is king.

www.marketingpilgrim.com/2008/04/social-media-marketing-beginners-guide.html

All social media sites have their own guides on how and why to use them and there are many unofficial guides published by users.

Example social media sites

The sites that are available change and grow in number all of the time. At the time of writing, two that have a very high profile and are used by many people in the Real Bread Campaign network are Twitter and Facebook, both of which are free to use.

Twitter – a microblogging site that allows users to send messages of up to 140 characters, which can include a link to images and more detailed information. Many journalists use Twitter and both bakers and Campaign staff have secured media coverage through Twitter.

The Real Bread Campaign posts messages on Twitter as **@realbread** and if you also use **#realbread** in the message, others searching for that label (known as a hashtag) will be able to see all messages containing it in one place.

Facebook – Can be used to set up personal profiles, as well as pages or groups for organisations. It allows users to publish details of events, upload pictures, has a notice board (referred to as a wall) on which the user and others can post messages, and allows users to send messages to others (referred to as friends or fans).

At the time of writing, without its own website, the E5 Bake House relies upon its Facebook page to inform customers (and potential customers) of its products, events and other news: www.facebook.com/pages/e5-bakehouse/132555766758130

The Campaign has a page on Facebook on which we publish updates on our work as well as links to information that might be of use and interest to our supporters: www.facebook.com/realbreadcampaign

Other social media sites include YouTube (primarily used for posting video clips), Flickr (a photo sharing site) and LinkedIn (a sort of online directory of business cards that allows you to send messages).

Media relations

This area of marketing is one often that small businesses either overlook or dismiss as too expensive, too time consuming or simply irrelevant. However, strong media relations can make the difference between your bakery being the one that is known, trusted and consequently frequented by people from miles around, or completely unheard of by anyone other than a small band of regular customers and the odd passer-by.

Unless your turnover is large enough to support hiring in a media/public relations company, this is something that you will need to look after yourself. The following will help you to run an effective media campaign.

If you do not actively seek media coverage to help grow your level of business, it still can be useful to have on file a selection of good quality pictures and an up-to-date sheet of general information about the bakery.

What and why?

The idea of media relations is building relationships with relevant journalists, editors, broadcasters, and bloggers so that when you have a story to tell, they are more likely to help you spread the word. It also means that when they are putting together a relevant news story or feature and need an interview, case study or picture, you are the first person/company that springs to mind.

Two of the key benefits of a news piece or feature in the local media as opposed to an advertisement are:

- Unlike adverts, articles are generally seen as independent and trustworthy opinions.
- They're free!

Media release

A media release (also known as a press release) is a very useful tool in persuading newspapers, magazines, TV/radio programmes and bloggers to help you communicate your messages to members of the public.

The pitch

Different people look for different things, all depending on the publication they work for, their particular 'newsdesk' (environment, rural, small business, local news etc.), and personal interests. You won't appeal to everyone every time you have something to say, but even modest media interest can lead to good coverage of your story.

To increase the chances of media coverage, ask yourself whether what are you offering is new, different (e.g. reviving ancient traditions or making/doing something that nobody else in the area does), local, of benefit to the community (e.g. fundraising for charity), or bringing local relevance to a wider issue – joining in with a national or international event or movement?

Considerations

Before you knuckle down to craft your media release, think:

- What is the **purpose** of the release? What am I trying to communicate?
- Who is my target **audience**?
- What **results** do I want to achieve? What do I want the audience to take away from the press release?
- What's my **hook**?
- When is the right **time**?
- Is a press release the best means by which to communicate this message to this audience?

Purpose - Why am I sending a release?

The reasons you might send a media release include to:

- Broadcast information.
- Increase awareness.
- Update target audiences.
- Call people to action.

A news release can be used for a host of reasons, e.g. when you launch a new initiative, put out findings of a survey/ research, win an award, secure sponsorship/funding, have an event to announce, or need to react to something that's happened.

Audience - To whom will my release speak?

Think about the audience of the publications (and particular columns/sections within them) to which you are sending the release and write for that audience.

With whom are you attempting to connect? An older member of the community who might like the idea of a traditional local tea room selling real crumpets, a businessman for whom a free range bacon sarnie on Real Bread on the way to work may be attractive; a mother who would be happy to pay you to take the kids off her hands for an afternoon of bread making in the school holidays…

Ideally, you'd tailor releases for every single recipient. Although this is not possible, if you're targeting different press sectors (e.g. local news, environment, community, rural affairs, bakery trade press, small business news, foodie press) with the same story, write adapted versions, rather than issuing one catch-all release.

Results - What results do I hope my release to produce?

Do you want people to come along and try the new bun you've created, turn up to an event, visit your new website, sign a petition, write to the local MP, take advantage of your baker's dozen incentive?

Outlining your goals before you start writing the release will help to give you direction when it you draft it.

The Hook

All releases need a strong hook, in other words, an element or angle that will give it the best chance of being picked by an editor/journalist as being of special interest to their audience.

Is what you're talking about:

- The first time something's happened?
- New?
- Significantly different?
- Hard-hitting?
- Of particular benefit to the audience of the publication in question?
- Making a wider issue relevant to a particular group – e.g. allowing participation in a national or international event or movement?
- Of human interest? This can sometimes be used to spark interest, as can association with high profile figures celebrities.

Timing

Old news is no news: news happens *now*. The time to put out a news release is as soon as you have a story to tell. Other types of release have less time pressure but everyone has a deadline. Research the deadlines of the media you are targeting to make sure you don't miss them - local papers might work a few days ahead but for glossy magazines, it can be several months.

You can struggle to secure coverage over school holidays (especially over the summer and Christmas) so, avoid all but news releases at these times.

If you have set a date/time before which you do not want a story to be published/broadcast, mark the release with details e.g. 'Embargoed until 9am, 20th December'. Embargoes are not legally binding but most journalists will respect them.

Alternatives

Do you feel that what you want to say will be of interest just to your business contacts or regular customers, rather than sectors of the wider public? If so, then other channels of communication that might be more appropriate than a press release, including:

- Your website.
- Your online forum.
- An email shot to your mailing list.
- Social media (e.g. Twitter or Facebook).

Structure and content

A media release has three main parts:

- Headline.
- Lead.
- Body.

Headline

First impressions count. This is your one line pitch to capture the reader's attention and act as bait to make him/her continue.

The headline should set out what you are about to say in snappy and unfrivolous language. Where the message is lighter in nature, however, wit might help your release to stand out, in which case the use of dreadful puns is a matter of personal choice.

Lead

Having cast your bait, you now need to hook the reader with all the Ws: the who, what, why, where, when, and how of the story. Keep to the facts and write no more than one or two lines or about 50 words.

Body

You've hooked the reader, now reel 'em in. Organise information from most important at the beginning through to progressively less important information: the reader won't have time to wade through several paragraphs to get to the meat of the story.

- What is the most important fact you wish to get across?
- Have you got strong statistics or other research results to support the story?
- Are there any other newsworthy aspects of your event, announcement, activity, product, or service?
- Is there a financial aspect? If it's positive (e.g. a significant discount or free anything) put it high up the release, perhaps even in the headline.

If your news story is the latest episode of a long saga or has a complex background, include a short summary of key developments further down the press release. Alternatively, these can be included in notes to editors.

Quotes

Journalists love to hear people's voices. To give the release (and news pieces it will help to generate) a human voice, include a short quote. This could be a notable person (such as a trusted expert, local figure or celebrity) or the business owner, which might well be you.

Images

'A picture paints…' and all that. If you have a strong, high-quality image, include it in the release as it can be the visual hook that helps to sell your story to the editor. To reduce the file size (files much over 5Mb can cause email crashes) of media releases that include photos, or logos, convert the finished document to a compressed PDF.

If you have a photo opportunity e.g. a celebrity, an opening, an eye-catching event or an unusual setting or prop, then make sure you highlight this. If the opportunity is particularly interesting, then it is worth writing a shorter release containing the when, where, what (and who) of the occasion, inviting newspaper and other media picture desks to take their own photos.

Format

- People in the media receive an endless stream of releases, so keep yours short and punchy. Two pages maximum, but one page is better.
- Ensure that your writing is clear, concise, and without unexplained jargon.
- Write about yourself in the third person: say 'the bakery' rather than 'we' (except in quotes).
- If sending by post or emailing as an attachment, the best format is A4 with borders of at least 2cm all around.
- Text should be justified and double spaced.
- Font is a matter of choice but to be taken seriously, and so as not to give the reader extra work, avoid cartoony or script fonts.
- Complete a paragraph on one page rather than carrying it over onto the next.
- Type 'more' at the bottom of the first page when the media release is more than one page long.
- After the body copy, insert the word ENDS.
- After this, include the date of the release, name and contact details (phone and/or email) for more information, plus a website, if applicable. If images or interviews are available, say so.

An optional final inclusion is 'Note(s) to the editor'. This is a summary of key facts that either are spread out through the release, or relevant background information that does not appear in it – e.g. a potted history of the bakery and any awards it has won.

Accuracy

A few very important points:

- Double check for spelling mistakes or other errors that a spellchecker wouldn't pick up on – a correctly spelled word but in the wrong place.
- Check that it's grammatically correct.
- Make sure that all of your facts (like dates) are correct and that any sources are quoted correctly.
- Even if you've read it ten times yourself, always ask someone else to proof read before sending.

The right contact

Although you are undoubtedly extremely busy running your business, it's worth taking a little time to find out the right contact at your local newspaper, news website, radio or TV station. If you don't make the effort to ensure that you send your release to the right person, you might not get featured, and if you send it to the wrong person, you definitely won't.

Research the subjects covered by particular TV stations, websites, radio stations and shows/sections within each. You also need to find the right person (or desk) to receive the release. The right contact depends on a number of factors, including the type of story you have, how many staff a publication/station has and how that organisation divides up its workload.

The news editor - may have local events in her/his remit

The features editor – might be interested in doing a profile on a long-running family business, recently started business or business that's doing something in an interesting/unusual way

Features writer – might be easier to get hold of than the features editor

Food editor – do you have a recipe to share? Do you bake something that is a local traditional speciality, quirky and/or new? Do you have a wood/coal fired oven? Are you the only bakery in your area doing something a certain way?

Forward planning desk – TV and radio stations usually have a person/team who note(s) details of events in a diary long in advance. If they are interested, they then contact you close (often very close) to the event to arrange to cover the story.

The editor – on smaller publications, the editor might be the best point of contact (they might not have features, news or food editors), who will then pass the story to the relevant journalist.

The deputy editor – can often be easier to get hold of than the main editor.

Specialist desk – are there dedicated reporters for business, rural affairs, local events, environment or other relevant area?

Building relationships

Establishing and building a relationship with the right contact can lead to being featured again. Don't expect a weekly column, but out of sight is out of mind and if you're known to a journalist or editor, there is more of a chance that he/she will think of you if a comment or example is needed for a related article in the future.

Post or email?

It's quick and easy to delete an email, but then it's also quick and easy to read one. Emails are also cheap to send and use no paper. The preference for receiving press releases by post or email varies from person to person – it pays to find out what each of your contacts prefers, especially if you are only sending your release to a few.

If you can, put your press release up on your website.

Follow up

Some stories have a life of their own – you send a release out and it flies, but these are the exception. Usually, securing coverage involves following up the release with a phone call.

Trade press

Generally, media interest in news such as a new staff member, refit of the bakehouse or trading results, will be limited to trade press, such as the British Baker magazine. Trade releases can be even shorter and less prosaic than media releases to the consumer press.

General background release

To save time having to repeat details of your business to editors/writers, it is useful to have a short general overview that you can send out. This only needs to be a few paragraphs, summing up details such as:

- A brief history of the bakery.
- Who the owners are.
- A mini-biography of the baker – including previous bakeries worked at.
- Any awards won.
- Future plans.
- Contact details.

It's important to keep this up to date.

Give the Campaign a plug

Whenever the opportunity arises, we'd love it if you gave the Real Bread Campaign a mention, please.

Let us know

If a publication, website or station picks up your story, please let us know. We'd love to share news of your success with others. If it's online, please email a link to realbread@sustainweb.org or if it's in print, it would be great if you could post us a copy of the article.

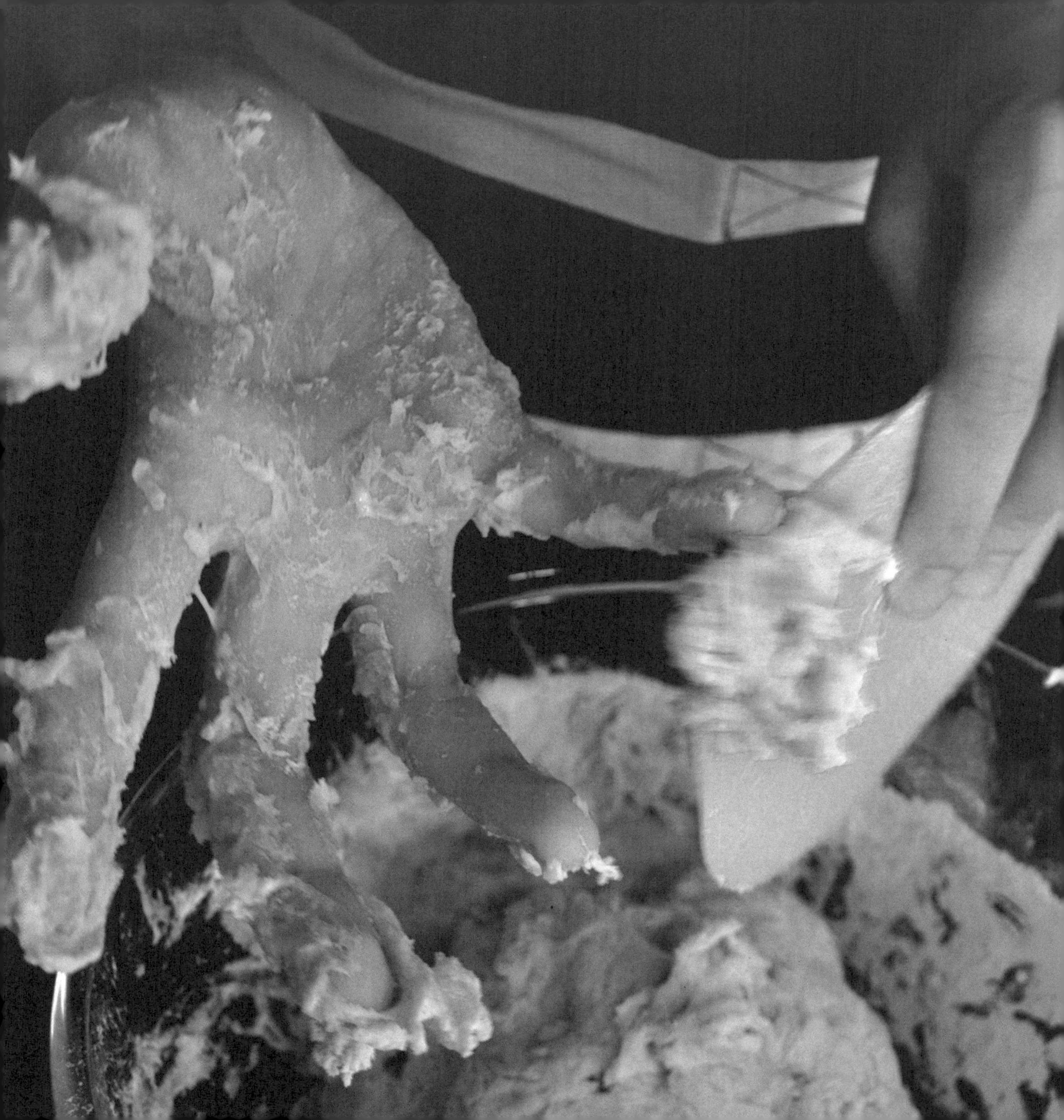

Courses and training

Many students on officially accredited and recognised bakery courses are sent by supermarkets and other industrial bakeries. As such, it appears that most, if not all, courses include topics not relevant to the Real Bread baker (e.g. activated dough development and the Chorleywood Bread Process) perhaps in favour of artisan baking skills and information.

The following are some of the places in which you can learn hands-on professional Real Bread skills. Some offer workshops in Community Supported Baking, as noted.

You can find details of more classes on the ever-growing courses page of our website.

The Bertinet Kitchen
12 St Andrew's Terrace, Bath. BA1 2QR
tel: 01225 445531
email: www.thebertinetkitchen.com/contact.php
web: www.thebertinetkitchen.com/programmes.php

Led by Richard Bertinet and his team, the hands-on bread making classes run from a one-day introduction, through to five-day courses looking at subjects such as sourdough, French and Italian breads. All classes are open to all abilities, but professional bakers are identified at the beginning of each course to make sure they learn in a way that will help them when they return to their bakeries and the tutor will try to cover anything specific that they wish to improve on. Private classes tailored to individual bakers can be arranged, either at The Bertinet Kitchen or at their bakeries.

Bread Matters
Macbiehill Farmhouse, Lamancha, West Linton,
Peeblesshire EH46 7AZ
tel: 01968 660449
email: andrew@breadmatters.com
web: www.breadmatters.com

Bread Matters is led by Andrew Whitley who started one of the UK's best known organic bakeries in the 1970s and is co-founder of the Real Bread Campaign. Bread Matters offers courses for everyone with a desire to produce Real Bread. Courses available for professional bakers and in baking for community.

The Handmade Bakery
14 Carr Lane, Slaithwaite, Yorkshire HD7 5AN
tel: 0789 403 6742
email: info@thehandmadebakery.coop
web: www.thehandmadebakery.coop/courses

One of the first Community Supported Bakeries in the country offers several courses a year, ranging from baking Real Bread at home through to setting up a Community Supported Bakery.

The Lighthouse Bakery School
Ockham, Dagg Lane, Ewhurst Green,
Robertsbridge, East Sussex, TN32 5RD
tel: 01580 831 271
email: liz@lighthousebakery.co.uk
web: www.lighthousebakery.co.uk

In addition to regular courses that are not specifically aimed at professionals, the Lighthouse Bakery offers bespoke courses for chefs and consultancy for people wanting to open bakeries.

Loaf Cookery School
Cotteridge, South Birmingham
tel: 07811 178272 (Tom)
email: tom@loafonline.co.uk
web: www.loafonline.co.uk/cookeryschool

A Community Supported Bakery, Loaf runs a one-day introduction to baking your own bread (Bread: back to basics), which covers all the essentials to help you get started with handmade artisan bread, and a two-day 'Simply Sourdough' course to take it that one step further. Tom's courses focus on bread, rather than business, but you might well be able to pick the brains of this social entrepreneur for CSB tips while you're with him.

Love Loaves
Wolvercote, Oxford
tel: 07886 280 800 (Dragan)
email: online form at www.loveloaves.biz/contact/
web: www.loveloaves.biz

Having set up their own micro-bakery at home to supply the local shop, Dragan and Penny have produced a Mini-Bakery Blueprint and run courses to share with others who want to learn how they did it.

Panary
Cann Mills, Shaftesbury, Devon, SP7 0BL
tel: 01722 711 760
email: info@panary.co.uk
web: www.panary.co.uk

Paul Merry has been involved with craft baking and masonry ovens for over thirty years, and has been teaching courses for fifteen years. He offers a range of one-, two- and three-day baking courses including British traditional, Italian, French and sourdough breads.

The Phoenix Bakery
6-7 St. Thomas Street, Weymouth, Dorset DT4 8EW
tel: 01305 767 894
email: phoenixbakery@hotmail.com
web: www.phoenixbakery.co.uk

The Monday Bakery School is for anyone wanting to improve their own baking skills, whilst The Phoenix Bakery's Apprenticeship Saturdays allow you to work the whole day as Aidan Chapman's apprentice and get a written report to enhance your CV.

The School of Artisan Food
Lower Motor Yard, Welbeck, Nottinghamshire S80 3LR
tel: 0845 520 1111
email: info@schoolofartisanfood.org
web: www.schoolofartisanfood.org/courses/findcourses/baking-courses

The school not only teaches practical and enjoyable ways to produce food, but also asks important questions about why food is produced in the way it is, what the alternatives are and what the future may look like. The school offers training ranging from one-day classes, through short courses, to a full one-year degree-level diploma, which covers all aspects of running a food business.

Shipton Mill
Shipton Mill, Frampton on Severn, Gloucestershire
tel: 01666 505050
email: fsmallman@shipton-mill.com
web: www.shipton-mill.com/the-bakery/baking-great-bread/bread-making-courses

The courses are extremely popular and Shipton Mill operates a waiting list. If you are interested in a place, email them your details and they will contact you when a space is available.

Wild Yeast Bakery
The Grange, Dean Road, Newnham on Severn, GL14 1HJ
tel: 0845 4580 060
email: simon@wildyeastbakery.co.uk
web: www.wildyeastbakery.co.uk

Participants learn about traditional bread making techniques, including how to use yeast with the overnight biga process, and how to cultivate wild yeast or sourdough cultures, to make a variety of breads. The course is run by Simon Michaels, who ran the bakery for three years.

Real Bread Bakers' Angels

As Real Bread Campaign members, professional bakers can call upon some of the country's most experienced and respected experts for advice. Simply post your questions in The Real Baker-e for one of our Bakers' Angels to answer.

http://groups.yahoo.com/group/realbreadcampaign/

Traditional oven-building

Here are the websites of just some of the places that offer courses in building earth/cob/clay ovens.

Dorset
www.cherrywoodproject.co.uk/earthoven.html
www.rivercottage.net/shop/product/build-and-bake

North Devon
www.wildpath.co.uk/blog-and-bushcraft-tutorials/item/24-how-to-build-an-earth-oven-course.html

Powys
www.earthovens.co.uk

Hackney
www.lowimpact.org/hackney_course_outline_earth_oven.htm

North Yorkshire
www.tastethewild.co.uk/earth_oven_28.html
www.realclayovens.co.uk/Cambridgeshire

Norfolk
www.edwardscobbuilding.com/index.php?p=PIZZAOVENS

Ingredient suppliers

Independent mills

Most mills produce a wide range of flours and many offer a bespoke service for commercial bakers. If you have specific questions (e.g. where the wheat was grown, about organic or 'conventional' farming, whether it was stoneground or roller milled, or if a sustainable source of energy was used) of any given flour, please check with the miller in question. Please also check with the miller about the ingredients in each flour - even some organic millers might add certain 'improvers' to some of their flours, which would put the resulting loaves outside the Campaign's definition of Real Bread.

The flour market in the UK is dominated by a handful of national and multinational companies. We don't have space to list all of those that remain independent but here are a few. See the *finding a local mill* section below the list for advice on tracking down others.

Bacheldre Watermill
Churchstoke, Montgomery, Powys SY15 6TE
Contact: Matt & Anne Scott
tel: 01588 620489
email: info@bacheldremill.co.uk
web: www.bacheldremill.co.uk

Range includes some stoneground, organic and local grain flours.

Denver Windmill
Denver, Downham Market, Norfolk PE38 0EG
Contact: Mark and Lindsay Abel
tel: 01366 384 009
email: enquiries@denvermill.plus.com
web: www.denvermill.co.uk

All flours stoneground from grain grown within sight of the mill.

Doves Farm Foods Ltd
Salisbury Road, Hungerford, Berkshire. RG17 0RF
Contact: Matt Long
tel: 01488 684880
email: mlong@dovesfarm.co.uk
web: www.dovesfarm.co.uk

Producers and suppliers of a range of organic flours, milled from combinations of UK and other grain. Range includes both stoneground and roller milled products.

Gilchesters Organics
Gilchesters Organic Farm, Hawkwell, Northumberland. NE18 0QL
Contact: Andrew and Sybille Wilkinson
tel: 01661 886 119
email: info@gilchesters.com
web: www.gilchesters.com

Stoneground flour from organic grain grown on their own land in Northumberland. Range includes spelt and heritage wheats.

Heygates Ltd
Bugbrooke Mills, Northampton NN7 3QH
tel: 01604 830381
email: pheygate@heygates.co.uk
web: www.heygates.co.uk/flourhome.html

Some flours milled from British wheat. Offers a bespoke service for commercial bakers.

Maple Farm Kelsale
Saxmundham, Suffolk IP17 2PL
tel: 01728 652000
email: info@maplefarmkelsale.co.uk
web: www.maplefarmkelsale.co.uk

Flour from organic rye, wheat and spelt grown and stone-milled on the farm in Suffolk

W&H Marriage
Chelmer Mills, New Street, Chelmsford, Essex CM1 1PN
tel: 01245 354455
email: floursales@marriagesmillers.co.uk
web: www.marriagesmillers.co.uk

Range includes some organic and some stoneground flours. Offers a bespoke service for commercial bakers.

FWP Matthews Ltd
Station Road, Shipton under Wychwood,
Chipping Norton, Oxon
tel: 01993 830342
email: sales@fwpmatthews.co.uk
web: www.fwpmatthews.co.uk

Some flours are organic and some are milled from British wheat.

Sharpham Park
Walton Nr Street Somerset BA16 9SA
tel: 01458 844 080
email: info@sharphampark.com
web: www.sharphampark.com

Stone mills 100% British spelt flour from its own organic farm.

Shipton Mill
Long Newnton, Tetbury, Gloucestershire. GL8 8RP
Contact: Fleur (small retail and general enquiries)
or Clive Mellum (trade enquiries only)
tel : 01666 505050
email : enquiries@shipton-mill.com or
cmellum@shipton-mill.com
web: www.shipton-mill.com

Range includes some stoneground and organic flours, some produced using UK-grown grain. Offers a bespoke service for commercial bakers.

N.R. Stoates & Sons
Cann Mills, Shatesbury, Dorset SP7 0BL
Contact: Michael Stoate
tel: 01747 852475
email: michael@stoatesflour.co.uk
web: www.stoatesflour.co.uk

Stoneground organic flour, some lines using grain grown locally to the mill.

Tamarisk Farm
West Bexington, Dorchester, Dorset DT2 9DF
Contact: Adam Simon
tel: 01308 897781
email: farm@tamariskfarm.co.uk
web: www.tamariskfarm.co.uk

Mills organic 100% wholemeal wheat (Maris Wigeon) and rye flours from grain grown on the farm.

G.R. Wright & Sons Ltd
Ponders End Mills, Enfield, Middlesex EN3 4TG
tel: 020 8344 6900
email: sales@wrightsflour.co.uk
web: www.wrightsflour.co.uk

Range includes some flours milled from 100% British wheat

Yorkshire Organic Millers
Hill Top Farm, Spaunton, Appleton-le-Moors,
York YO62 6TR
tel: 01751 417 351
email: organicmillers@btconnect.com
web: www.yorkshireorganicmillers.co.uk

Produces stoneground flour using only locally grown organic grain (wheat and spelt), all milled on site and mostly sold locally.

Finding a local mill

One of the following organisations might be able to point you to a mill near you:

The Traditional Cornmillers Guild
Represents many of our remaining wind and water-powered mills that produce stoneground flour, some using locally grown grain.
www.tcmg.org.uk

Society for the Protection of Ancient Buildings
Has a mills section, some members of which produce flour.
www.spab.org.uk/spab-mills/

National Association of British and Irish Millers (NABIM)
Represents the interests of the UK and Irish milling industries. Their members include both independent millers and the larger companies that dominate the market.
www.nabim.org.uk

Organic Ingredients

Suppliers of organic ingredients include:

Community Foods
Micross, Brent Terrace, London NW2 1LT
tel: 0208 450 9411
web: www.communityfoods.co.uk

Harley Foods
Blindcrake Hall, Blindcrake, Cockermouth,
Cumbria CA13 0QP
tel: 01900 823037

Infinity Foods Co-op Ltd
Franklin Road, Portslade, Brighton,
East Sussex BN41 1AF
tel: 01273 424060
web: www.infinityfoods.co.uk

Rasanco
The Estate Office, Sutton Scotney, Hants SO21 3JW
tel: 01962 761935
web: www.rasanco.com

Suma Wholefoods
Unit G15, Lowfields Business Park, Lacy Way,
Elland, W. Yorks HX5 9DB
tel: 01422 313861
web: www.suma.co.uk

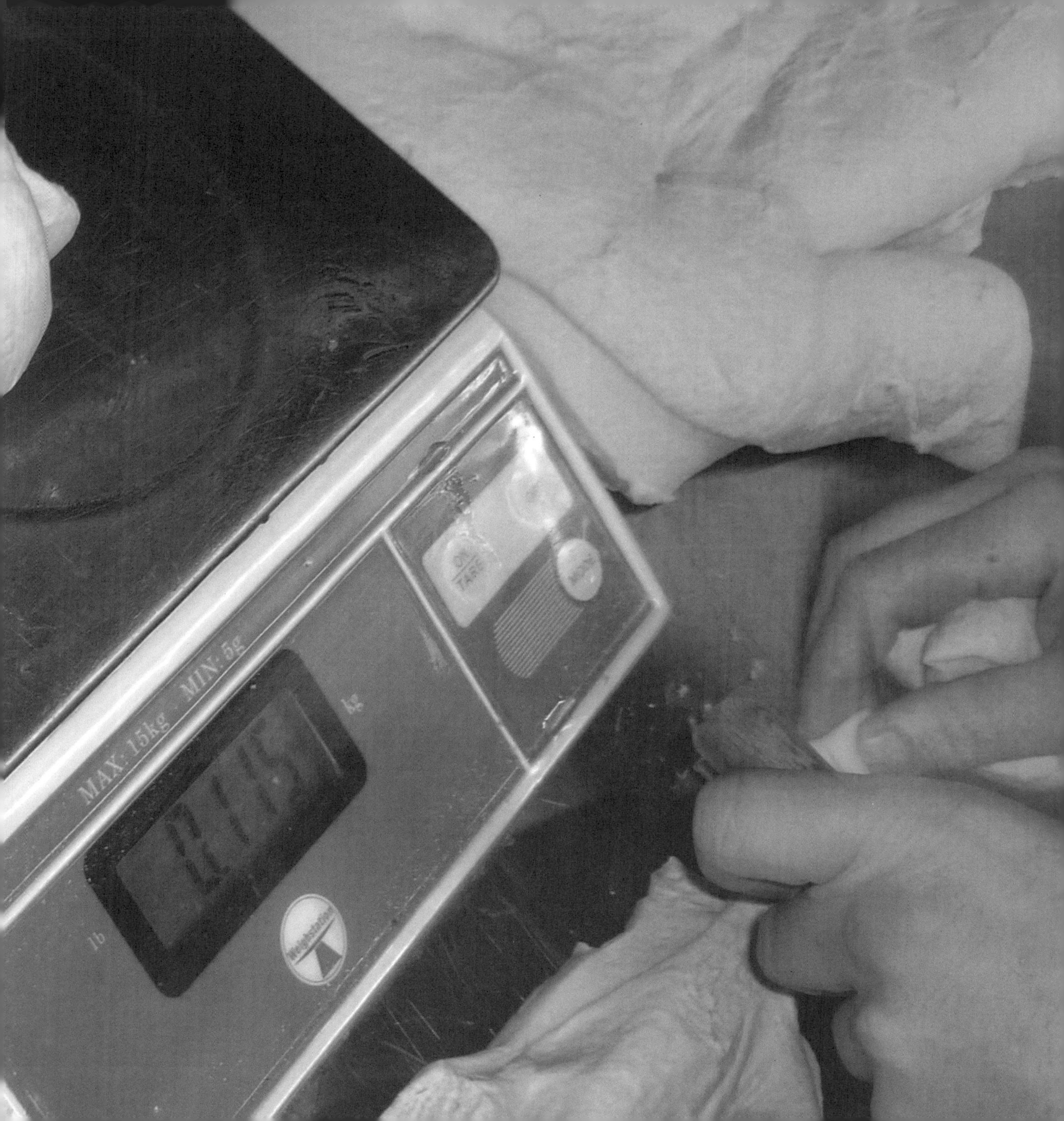
MAX: 15kg MIN: 5g
kg
lb
TARE

Equipment suppliers

The following are just some of the companies that supply new (and in some cases used) professional baking equipment, ancillary items and packaging. Some specialise (e.g. wood-fired ovens), while others are more general. Please visit the relevant website for details of what each supplies.

Armstrong Brick Ovens
tel: 07989 410528
web: www.armstrongbrickovens.co.uk

Bakery Bits
web: www.bakerybits.co.uk

Becketts
Fir Street, Heywood, Lancashire, OL10 1NP
tel: 01706 364103
email: info@becketts.co.uk
web: www.becketts.co.uk

Belmont Bakery Machinery
The Factory, Watermead Works, Slater Lane, Bolton, Lancashire BL1 2TE
tel: 01204 370743
email: www.bakerymachinery.co.uk/contact/
web: www.bakerymachinery.co.uk

The Bertinet Kitchen
12 St Andrew's Terrace, Bath, BA1 2QR
tel: 01225 445531
email: info@thebertinetkitchen.com
web: www.thebertinetkitchen.com/shop/bread_making

Charlotte Packaging Ltd
The Forge, Woodend Farm, Cromhall, Wotton-under-Edge, Gloucestershire GL12 8AA
tel: 01454 269669
email: info@charlottepackaging.com
web: www.charlottepackaging.com

Ernst Birnbaum Company (AKA brotformen.de)
Am Mühlgraben 5, D - 04779 Wermsdorf/Ortsteil Mahlis, Kreis Torgau-Oschatz/Sachsen, Germany
Tel: +49-(0)34 364-522 87 (N.B. the website says 'don't call, as no one speaks English there')
email: kontakt@brotformen.de
web: www.bannetons.com

Brook Food Processing Equipment
Channing House, Mart Road Trading Estate, Minehead, Somerset. TA24 5BJ
tel: 01643 704 541
email: www.brookfood.co.uk/contact_us.php
web: www.brookfood.co.uk

Creeds (Southern) Ltd
New Street, Waddesdon, Aylesbury, Bucks HP18 0LR
tel: 01296 658849
email: buy@creeds.uk.com
web: www.creeds.uk.com

Eastwood Sales
Shakespeare House, Ipswich Road, Ardleigh, Colchester, Essex CO7 7QW
tel: 01206 230583
email: enquiries@bakerymachinesales.com
web: www.bakerymachinesales.co.uk

Lincat
Whisby Road, Lincoln LN6 3QZ
tel: 01522 875555
email: sales@lincat.co.uk
web: www.lincat.co.uk

Modern Baking Systems
Olympia House, 26 Clothier Road, Brislington, Bristol BS4 5PS
tel: 0117 9779494
email: sales@modernbaking.co.uk
web: www.modernbaking.co.uk

Nisbets
Fourth Way, Avonmouth, Bristol, BS11 8TB
tel: 0845 140 5555
email; sales@nisbets.co.uk
web: www.nisbets.co.uk

Panary
Cann Mills, Shaftesbury, Dorset, SP7 0BL
tel: 01747 823711
email: info@panary.co.uk
web: www.panary.co.uk

R.M Royster Bakery Engineers
Unit C, Miller Street, Heywood, Lancashire OL10 4HX
tel: 01706 622144
email: mikeroyster@bakerymachineryuk.com or ronroyster@bakerymachineryuk.com
web: www.bakerymachineryspares.co.uk

D T Saunders Ltd
103 London Road, Leicester LE2 0PF
tel: 0116 2542121
email: sales@bakeryequipment.co.uk
web: www.bakeryequipment.co.uk

Scobie & McIntosh (Bakery Engineers) Ltd
Oakwell Business Centre, Dark Lane, Birstall, West Yorkshire WF17 9LW
tel: 01924 432 940
email: sales@scobie-equipment.co.uk
web: www.scobie-equipment.co.uk/

Target Catering Equipment
Unit 1 Ashville Trading Estate, Bristol Road, Gloucester GL2 5EU
tel: 01452 410447
email: david.pedrette@targetcatering.co.uk
web: www.targetcatering.co.uk

Vegware
PO Box 27119, Edinburgh EH10 5WN
tel: 0845 643 0406
email: info@vegware.com
web: www.vegware.com

Second hand

Some bakers (notably those starting very small-scale operations or Community Supported Bakeries) have found the web-based communities useful in picking up second-hand equipment.

In all cases, you must seek and take the advice of the service you are using regarding safety when meeting to make an exchange, or concerning other aspects of your purchase, such as electrical safety or stolen goods. The Real Bread Campaign/Sustain cannot take responsibility for using any of these services, or for any consequences of doing so.

These are some of the sites that could allow you to find (or pass on) used baking equipment. Some offer free advertisements and even offer the opportunity to pick up or pass on items and services without money changing hands. Others are sales-based and deal in both new and used equipment.

www.dontdumpthat.com
www.ebay.co.uk
www.uk.freecycle.org
www.ilovefreegle.org
www.gumtree.com
www.letsallshare.com
www.ooffoo.com
www.vskips.co.uk

traditional home winemaking
paul and ann turner
Katz
wild fermentation
The Flavor, Nutrition, and Craft of Live-Culture Foods
CHELSEA GREEN
real flavours
the handbook of gourmet & deli ingredients
Glynn Christian
REINHART
The Bread Baker's Apprentice
TEN SPEED PRESS
Hamelman
BREAD
A Baker's Book of Techniques and Recipes
WILEY
DOUGH
Simple Contemporary Bread • Richard Bertinet
WING and SCOTT
THE BREAD BUILDERS
HEARTH LOAVES and MASONRY OVENS
Dan Lepard
The handmade loaf
MITCHELL BEAZLEY
andrew whitley
bread matters
the state of modern bread and a definitive guide to baking your own
4th
BUILDING A WOOD-FIRED OVEN FOR BREAD AND PIZZA • TOM JAINE
River Cottage Handbook Bread
self-sufficiency
Cheese Making
Rita Ash
SAINSBURY'S HEALTHY·EATING·COOKBOOKS
Breads

Bookshelf

Here are just some books that the serious Real Bread baker might find interesting and informative, some more for academic purposes, others for recipes and other practical matters.

Several are available in later editions and/or paperback. If a book is out of print, you might be able to find a copy through a library (though you'll have to ask them to order you a copy), a second-hand/antiquarian bookshop, and in some cases, you might find some or all of the text is available online.

Manna: A Comprehensive Treatise on Bread Manufacture, W. Banfield, Maclaren & Sons (1947)

The Bread Bible, R. Barenbaum, Norton (2003)

Bread Street: The British baking bloomer?, Mel Barrett, Sustain publications (2004) - available to download from www.sustainweb.org/publications/order/100/

Dough and **Crust**, Richard Bertinet, Kyle Cathie (2005 and 2007)

The Master Bakers Book of Breadmaking (3rd edition), J. Brown (ed.), National Association of Master Bakers Brown, (1996)

The Taste of Bread, R. Calvel, J. MacGuire and R. Wirtz, Aspen (2001)

The Technology of Breadmaking (2nd edition), S. Cauvain, and L. Young, L. S. Springer – Verlag (2007)

Practical Bakery, Connelly, P., Pittam, M. Hodder & Stoughton (1997)

English Bread and Yeast Cookery, Elizabeth David, Allen Lane (1977)

Build Your Own Earth Oven: A Low-Cost Wood-Fired Mud Oven; Simple Sourdough Bread; Perfect Loaves (3rd Edition), Kiko Denzer and Hannah Field, Hand Print Press (2007)

How Baking Works: exploring the fundamentals of baking science (2nd edition), Paula Figoni, John Wiley & Sons (2008)

Artisan Baking, Maggie Glezer, Workman Publishing (2000)

Bread: A Baker's Book of Techniques and Recipes, Jeffrey Hamelman, John Wiley & Sons (2004)

Breadcraft, JR Irons, Hudson and Stracey (1934)

Six Thousand Years of Bread: Its Holy and Unholy History, H.E. Jacob, The Lyons Press (1997)

The Modern Baker, Confectioner and Caterer, John Kirkland, Gresham Books (1907)

Bread Alone: Bold Fresh Loaves From Your Own Hands, Daniel Leader and Judith Blahnik, Morrow (1993)

Local Breads: Sour Doughs and Whole Grain Recipes From Europe's Best Artisan Bakers, Daniel Leader and Lauren Chattman, Norton (2007)

The Handmade Loaf, Dan Lepard, Mitchell Beazley (2004)

McGee on Food & Cooking, Harold McGee, Hodder and Stoughton (2004)

The Bread Baker's Apprentice, Peter Reinhart, Ten Speed Press (2001)

Crust and Crumb: Master Formulas for Serious Bread Bakers, Peter Reinhart, Ten Speed Press

Whole Grain Breads, Peter Reinhart, Ten Speed Press (2007)

River Cottage Handbook No. 3: Bread, Daniel Stevens, Bloomsbury Publishing (2009)

Bread Matters, Andrew Whitley, Fourth Estate (2006)

The Bread Builders: Hearth Loaves and Masonry Ovens, D. Wing and A. Scott, Chelsea Green (1999)

This list continues to grow on our website and you can find an enormous list of bread books at http://breadmaking.iilu.com/books-0001.shtml

More useful links

You can find many links to potentially useful websites on the courses, companions and events pages of our website at www.realbreadcampaign.org

Moulding loaves

Boules
www.youtube.com/watch?v=45z18TtFijU
www.youtube.com/watch?v=WhJUoi7SV7s

Tin loaf
www.youtube.com/user/TheFrenchBaker#p/a/u/1/dmLryYC25dQ
www.youtube.com/watch?v=CmQ2hbK7Nl4

Rolls
www.youtube.com/watch?v=igOQ444V84U

Baguettes
www.youtube.com/watch?v=OI-WstoakmQ

Torpedo
www.youtube.com/watch?v=kuwUdxGfFLk

Various
www.youtube.com/watch?v=7MVHDdDtuRc
www.youtube.com/user/FCIIBP#p/c/7CB6E6874F63E48A

Business and enterprise

Business Link
The government's free business advice and support service, available online and through local advisers. Use 'bakery product retail' as a search term to find summaries of relevant regulations, licences, British and European standards and contacts.
www.businesslink.gov.uk

The National Association of Master Bakers
Provides information, advice, training and support for its members in the craft baking sector.
www.masterbakers.co.uk

Enterprise UK
Founded in 2004 by the British Chamber of Commerce, the Confederation of British Industry, the Institute of Directors and the Federation of Small Businesses, funded mostly by what is now called the Department for Business, Innovation & Skills. Aims to '...reach out to new people of all ages and backgrounds, fresh thinkers who spot opportunities, apply entrepreneurial talents and overcome the obstacles to make ideas happen.'
www.enterpriseuk.org

Bakers Benevolent Society
Provides: "...welfare and care to retired members of the baking industry and allied trades, including their dependants, through its provision of sheltered accommodation and financial support."
www.bakersbenevolent.co.uk

Alliance and Leicester
A page of industry sector notes for those considering starting a bakery.
www.alliance-leicestercommercialbank.co.uk/bizguides/full/baker/parkes-sector_trends.asp

SmallBusiness.co.uk
Site includes tips on sources of funding and grants for small businesses.
www.smallbusiness.co.uk/channels/small-business-finance/government-grants/guides-and-tips/

British Chambers of Commerce (BCC)
www.britishchambers.org.uk

Confederation of British Industry (CBI)
www.cbi.org.uk

Federation of Small Businesses (FSB)
www.fsb.org.uk

School for Start Ups
www.schoolforstartups.co.uk

Enterprise Nation
www.enterprisenation.com

Social Enterprise Coalition
www.socialenterprise.org.uk

Funding

Some of the following also offer workshops to help you find and secure funding.

The Soil Association
www.soilassociation.org/Takeaction/Getinvolvedlocally/Communitysupportedagriculture/Fundingopportunities/tabid/226/Default.aspx

Fresh Ideas Network
www.freshideas.org.uk/funding-tips/index.htm

Local Action on Food Network
www.sustainweb.org/localactiononfood/local_food_funding/

FunderFinder
www.funderfinder.org.uk

Funding Central
www.fundingcentral.org.uk

Grant Finder
www.grantfinder.co.uk

Media relations

The Media Trust
www.mediatrust.org/training-events/training-resources/online-guides-1

Civicus
www.civicus.org/new/media/Handling%20the%20Media.pdf

Community Supported Baking

Co-operatives UK

Assists co-operatives and other third sector organisations to become incorporated and offer long-term governance and legal support for those co-operatives that are members of Co-operatives UK.

www.cooperatives-uk.coop

The Soil Association

Produces a lot of material and information to support Community Supported Agriculture. Much of this may be of interest and/or use to those looking at starting a CSB, including A Share in The Harvest: An action manual for community supported agriculture.

www.soilassociation.org/LinkClick.aspx?fileticket=gi5uOJ9swil%3d&tabid=204

Making Local Food Work

An initiative managed by the Plunkett Foundation and funded by the Big Lottery Fund to explore community enterprise approaches to connecting land and people through food. www.makinglocalfoodwork.co.uk/about/fcbg/index.cfm

Food Co-ops

Provides detailed advice for local food co-operatives. Their Food Co-ops Toolkit is primarily aimed at groups working with fruit, vegetables and other wholefoods, but much of the information would be equally relevant to a bread group.

www.foodcoops.org

f3

f3 is a co-operative Community Interest Company providing consultancy services to the local food sector. It can offer up to five days free consultancy to community food enterprises in England, under the Making Local Food Work programme.

www.localfood.org.uk

Community Food Hubs

A paper published by the Food Supply and Distribution project, which is investigating community-led approaches to building more robust and sustainable food systems. The project is run by Sustain as part of the Lottery-funded Making Local Food Work programme.

www.sustainweb.org/pdf/Building_Sustainable_Community_Food_Hub.pdf

SETAS

'The UK's only one-stop marketplace for Social Enterprise Training and Support.'

www.setas.co.uk

Fresh Ideas

'The Fresh Ideas Network supports community food projects which aim to make healthy/local food more easily available, accessible and affordable to local communities, particularly in areas of disadvantage.'

www.freshideas.org.uk

The Co-operative Enterprise Hub

'The Co-operative Enterprise Hub aims to expand the co-operative economy by creating strong, ethically-led businesses with a deep sense of social responsibility. It offers a package of advice, training and finance to help new and existing co-operatives become more sustainable businesses.'

www.co-operative.coop/enterprisehub

Employment

The Real Baker-e
The forum for Real Bread Campaign members in which we encourage bakeries looking for staff or apprentices and people looking for work or an apprenticeship to post details.
http://groups.yahoo.com/group/realbreadcampaign/

British Baker
Carries job adverts.
www.bakeryinfo.co.uk

Dan Lepard
Has a page dedicated to bakery jobs.
www.danlepard.com/section/jobs/

Regulation and legislation

This is only a guide and you should check with the relevant local authority or governmental department for definitive advice on the current legislation.

The Bread and Flour Regulations 1998
www.legislation.gov.uk/uksi/1998/141/contents/made

Employers Liability (Compulsory Insurance) Act 1969 and Regulations 1998
www.opsi.gov.uk/si/si1998/19982573.htm
www.hse.gov.uk/pubns/hse40.pdf

Consumer Protection Act 1987
www.opsi.gov.uk/acts/acts1987/pdf/ukpga_19870043_en.pdf
www.legislation.gov.uk/si/si1987/Uksi_19871680_en_1.htm

General Product Safety Regulations 2005
www.opsi.gov.uk/si/si2005/20051803.htm

Trades Description Act 1968
www.berr.gov.uk/files/file8156.pdf

The Consumer Protection from Unfair Trading Regulations 2008
www.oft.gov.uk/shared_oft/business_leaflets/cpregs/oft1008.pdf
www.opsi.gov.uk/si/si2008/pdf/uksi_20081277_en.pdf

Supply of Goods and Services Act 1982
www.opsi.gov.uk/revisedstatutes/acts/ukpga/1982/cukpga_19820029_en_1

The Equalities Act 2010
This replaces many previous acts, covering issues including age, disability, gender reassignment, race, religion or belief, sex, sexual orientation, marriage and civil partnership and pregnancy and maternity.
www.equalities.gov.uk/equality_bill.aspx

Fire Precautions Act 1971 (workplace), Regulations 1997 and Amendment 1999
www.archive.official-documents.co.uk/document/fire/intro.htm
www.opsi.gov.uk/RevisedStatutes/Acts/ukpga/1971/cukpga_19710040_en_1

The Electricity at Work Regulations 1989
www.opsi.gov.uk/si/si1989/Uksi_19890635_en_1.htm

The Reporting of Injuries, Diseases and Dangerous Occurrences Regulations 1995
www.opsi.gov.uk/SI/si1995/Uksi_19953163_en_1.htm

The Provision and Use of Work Equipment Regulations 1998
www.opsi.gov.uk/si/si1998/19982306.htm

Health and Safety at Work etc. Act 1974
www.opsi.gov.uk/RevisedStatutes/Acts/ukpga/1974/cukpga_19740037_en_1

Employing under 18s
www.direct.gov.uk/en/YoungPeople/Workandcareers/Yourrightsandresponsibilitiesatwork/DG_066272

Traditional ovens

The Clay Oven
A comprehensive step-by-step online guide (also offered as a PDF to download), with FAQs and links to other guides, courses and related websites.
http://clayoven.wordpress.com/

Kiko Denzer
Blog by the author of Build Your Own Earth Oven
http://kikodenzer.blogspot.com/

Mother Earth News
A guide by Kiko Denzer
www.motherearthnews.com/Do-It-Yourself/2002-10-01/Build-Your-Own-Wood-Fired-Earth-Oven.aspx

The Thoughtful Bread Company
www.thethoughtfulbreadcompany.com/building_clay_oven.php

Traditional Oven
www.traditionaloven.com

Masonry Stove Builders
Guides and plans for a range of traditional ovens and links to related sites
http://heatkit.com/html/bakeoven.htm

Miscellaneous

Environment Agency
www.environment-agency.gov.uk

Health & Safety Executive (HSE)
www.hse.gov.uk

Institution of Occupational Safety and Health (IOSH)
www.iosh.co.uk

Royal Society for the Prevention of Accidents (RoSPA)
www.rospa.com

Appendix 1:
Community Supported Bakery start-up checklist

If there is more than one person setting up a CSB, all those involved need to decide and agree upon its aims and set up.

It helps for each party to decide and express clearly what they are looking for. This tick list is intended to help a group decide what it wants from its CSB. This list is not exhaustive and you may have extra or different questions of your own.

A theoretical example:

We are a community group of about 12 active people. We want to develop a new project. We want to provide Real Bread to people in town X. We want to provide honestly priced and accessible Real Bread to low income households, as well as the wider population of town X. We want opportunities to get our hands doughy in the bakehouse and can offer about 20 hours per week volunteer time, but none of us wants to be a full time baker – we want to work with a skilled Real Bread baker. We think we can raise about £2000 as a donation to the bakery to help with set up costs. We think there will be about 50 people wanting a weekly loaf and we are happy to commit to a month at a time. We think about 50% of people would pay in advance for six months.

We are seeking a baker to work in partnership with us to meet our needs.

	Yes	No	Not important
We want to buy a bakehouse			
We want to rent a bakehouse			
We want to set up a homebakery			
We want to employ a professional Real Bread baker			
We want one or more of our members to learn the skills to be the CSB's baker(s)			
It is important that the bakehouse has a shop attached			
We want to supply Real Bread by retail/wholesale/subscription			
We want to use locally milled flour			
We want to use locally grown grain			
There are other factors about the Real Bread that are important (e.g. sourdough, organic, particular types of grain, wood fired oven)			
We want to make a sense of community through the bakery			
We want to make Real Bread available in a local community that doesn't have it			
We want to provide honestly priced Real Bread to those who most need it			
We want the bakery to provide a learning or work place for disabled people			
We want the bakery to provide a learning or work place for other groups (e.g. younger/older people wanting skills to help get into paid employment, children)			
We want to pay the baker well			
We could provide labour (in building/refurbishing the bakery)			
We want to help the bakery with our skills (e.g. marketing, accounts, selling etc.)			
We could provide capital to the bakery as a gift (e.g. for new oven)			
We could provide capital to the bakery as a loan			
We could provide capital to the bakery as an investment e.g. shares in the enterprise			
We want the bakery to be located in (or within X miles of) [place]			
We want our bread to be home delivered			
We want to set up a number of hubs from which subscribers collect their loaves			
Subscribers need to be willing to commit to a month's / six months' / a year's supply of bread			
Subscribers need to be willing to pay in advance for their order			
We want to offer a delivery service to			
Other…			

Appendix 2:
Basic food hygiene instruction form

Employer/business name . . . .

Name of employee/volunteer . . . .

Date started work . . . .

Keep yourself clean and wear clean clothing

Always wash your hands thoroughly:

- before handling food.
- after visiting the toilet.
- after handling raw foods or waste.
- before starting work.
- after every break.
- after blowing your nose.

Tell your supervisor, before commencing work, of any skin, nose, throat, stomach or bowel trouble or infected wound. YOU ARE BREAKING THE LAW IF YOU DON'T.

Ensure cuts and sores are covered with a waterproof, high visibility dressing and avoid unnecessary handling of food.

Do not smoke, eat or drink in a food room and never cough or sneeze over food.

Clean as you go and keep all equipment and surfaces clean.

If you see something wrong tell your supervisor.

Follow any safety instructions either on food packaging or from your supervisor.

Do not prepare food too far in advance (only applicable to those cooking food).

Keep perishable food either refrigerated or piping hot (only applicable to those cooking food).

Keep the preparation of raw and cooked food separate (only applicable to those cooking food).

When reheating foods ensure it gets piping hot (only applicable to those cooking food).

Follow any food safety instructions on food packaging or from your supervisor or Manager.

I have received training and understand the above instructions:

Signed . . . .

Appendix 3:
Thinking about your Real Bread

By Campaign working party member, Clare Marriage, Marketing Director of Doves Farm Food.

The more we can talk about our bread experiences, the more we can help others to understand why Real Bread is so good and why we need to campaign for it.

What does Real Bread look and taste like? By encouraging everyone to ask questions and start talking about bread we can open up the debate.

How does bread look in the shop? Does every loaf look identical and uniform in shape and size? Are there slight quirky variations to the shape and look of the bread? Perhaps it was wrapped in a series of identical bags, sitting on a shelf or piled into a basket.

How does bread feel when you touch it? Did the loaf appear large and fluffy or solid when you picked it up? How did any wrapping feel? Is the loaf generally soft and squidgy to touch, or crisp and crusty, or perhaps firmer and heavier?

How can the crust of a loaf vary? Are all the loaves identical and even in colour or are there variations to the external appearance, perhaps caused from the oven? Has the loaf been marked by the baker, or dusted with flour, or glazed to give it character? Does the crust impart a distinctive character to the loaf, or is it insignificant, or perhaps there is no crust?

What is bread like on the inside? Is the crumb soft, light and spongy, or does it have a web structure with large open holes, is it like cake in texture or perhaps it has a close, dense crumb? Can you see whole grains or flakes, or other ingredients in the bread?

What does bread smell like? Can you smell the grain the bread is made with, or are other smells stronger? Vinegar, malt or some flavourings? Is there a slight sour smell, or perhaps a strong one, or no smell at all. Did you hold a slice of bread up to your nose and smell deeply?

How does the bread feel in your mouth? Is the bread dry, limp and lifeless, or firm but not stiff, or just solid and heavy. Is the slice of bread difficult to bite through, does it stick to your teeth or is it pleasantly chewy. Could you tell the difference between the crust and the crumb?

What does bread taste like? Is there any flavour or is it rather bland? Can you taste the grain and anything you had previously smelled, such as vinegar or a flavour. Was there an aftertaste of salt, or malt? Would you enjoy eating the bread on its own or would that be rather boring?

How easy is bread to prepare? Can you cut a thin slice easily and without the loaf collapsing or was the bread ready sliced? Would a thick slice be undesirable? Would the bread taste better torn into pieces rather than sliced?

How do you know what is in bread? What information were you given about the bread at the point of purchase? How do you know what ingredients went into the bread and how it was made? How do you know if a loaf is going to be white bread, or wholemeal or made with unusual ingredients? Is there a label or packaging that gives a full list of ingredients?

How do you know who made the bread? Was your loaf packed under a specific brand name? Did the baker who sold the bread make it or buy it in? Did the baker display information about his baking methods? Was the bread made according to any known quality standards?

How can I tell if I am buying Real Bread? Did you ask the baker if his bread was freshly baked today and if he used anything other than flour, water and yeast for his bread?

References

1. Personal communication, David Smith, National Association of Master Bakers, 2002, cited by Barrett, Mel in Bread Street, Sustain Publications, 2004. Figures also quoted by Joanna Blythman in The Ecologist, 1st September 2004 http://ecologist.testing.net-genie.co.uk/investigations/food_and_farming/82824/special_report_supermarkets_bread.html (accessed January 2011)
2. Sacks, J. Public spending for public benefit, New Economics Foundation, London, July 2005
3. USDA Nutrient Database, SR 17, 2004
4. www.food.gov.uk/news/newsarchive/2010/jul/bakers 8 July 2010 (accessed January 2011)
5. www.greenpeace.org.uk/forests/faq-palm-oil-forests-and-climate-change (accessed January 2011)
6. www.nhs.uk/chq/pages/2145.aspx?categoryid=51&subcategoryid=167
7. www.ica.coop/coop/principles.html (accessed January 2011)
8. Social Enterprise: A Strategy for Success, Department of Trade and Industry, 2002

You can find links and references to more relevant articles and research at www.realbreadcampaign.org

Knead to Know has been produced with the support of:

LOTTERY FUNDED

BIG LOTTERY FUND

Local Food

Sheepdrove Trust

sustain

the alliance for better food and farming

Copyright notice

Disclaimer

Knead to Know is not definitive, is intended to provide guidance only and should not be taken as legal advice – this applies especially to notes on legislation. Awareness of, and compliance with, all parts of the most up-to-date versions of all relevant legislation relevant to running a safe bakery, is your responsibility and you should check with the relevant authorities to ensure that you fulfil these obligations. Sustain cannot be held responsible for the results of following (or not following) any suggestions contained in *Knead to Know*.

In line with Sustain policy, the Real Bread Campaign does not offer endorsement to any organisation, individual, product or service. Inclusion in *Knead to Know* does not imply any such endorsement. The views expressed in this publication are those of the respective authors and not necessarily of the Campaign or Sustain.

We have made every effort to ensure accuracy of the information provided and whilst we apologise for any errors or omissions, cannot be held responsible for any consequences that might arise as a result.

Should you have any feedback that you feel would enhance any future editions of *Knead to Know*, please send it to realbread@sustainweb.org